The Creator's Manifesto!

—Kathy Joy, Author

Reading this book made me feel more alive than I have in a long time.

—Sam, Engineer

This is it!!! This is the book I've been waiting for to bring clarity to my role and mandate as a creative. I create because God creates. He has ordained this work of creating within specific parameters. He gives boundaries and inspiration and direction to the creative process. These things and many more are what I have learned from reading this wonderful book. Whether you are on the beach or taking a lunch break at work, this book is a must read for anyone wanting to understand where the creative process begins and ends. It is validating to those who struggle to be recognized for their creative work as well as challenging to those who think they aren't creative. Don't miss this gem.

—Charmayne Hafen, Author

Laura Bartnick's writing will make anyone change the way they look at their talents, no matter what they are. She demonstrates, and with compelling Biblical references, how our artistic soul is a breath of God, a medium in which we encounter God and bring more life into the world. I enjoyed the simplicity of style and the depth of thought. The Biblical commentaries are spot on, relevant, and very inspiring. BEING CREATIVE is written in a down-to-earth, friendly style that delivers the core message with force. This book will help you understand why you have the gifts you have and how to use them. It's a book about being connected to God as a creative and finding meaning in the work one does as a creative. A very inspiring read.

—Rumoald Dzemo

BEING CREATIVE: is one of the best things I have read about creativity. Here is a book that unveils the startling intersection between art and spirituality, a book about life, about work and dignity, and about God working in us. In fact, it can be read as the spirituality of the creative person, a book that brilliantly showcases God's centrality in the creative process, demonstrating how we dance to the mystical tunes of the Creator, imitating Him in one of the aspects of our being — co-creators.
Filled with powerful insights and spiritual lessons, this book is designed to help readers — creative persons — reconnect with their craft and with themselves, and ultimately with the source of all inspiration.
Written in a friendly, warm tone, BEING CREATIVE makes the reader feel a deep sense of belonging.
The book offers a path toward fulfillment and purpose, featuring many Biblical references that will help readers develop a strong awareness of the sacredness of their creative endeavors.
Laura Bartnick knows how to speak to the reader's heart, using words that inspire and empower, and bringing readers to her point of view with compelling arguments. I enjoyed the anecdotes and how the author weaves her personal experiences into the story. If you are a creative, this book is for you. It will help you redefine why you ache to do what you are passionate about, and it will offer tools to make your work a success. It's a must-read.

—Arya Fomonyuy

BEING CREATIVE

Laura Bartnick

Capture Books

Publisher's Cataloging-In-Publication Data
(Prepared by The Donohue Group, Inc.)

Names: Bartnick, Laura.
Title: Being Creative / Laura Bartnick.
Description: Littleton, Colorado : Capture Books, [2021]
Identifiers: ISBN 978-1-951084-39-4 (paperback) | ISBN
    978-1-951084-40-0 (case laminate) | ISBN978-1-
    951084-41-7 (ebook)
Subjects: LCSH: Artists--Religious life. | Creative ability--
    Religious aspects--Christianity. | Christian life. | God
    (Christianity)
Classification: LCC BV4596.A78 B37 2021 (print) | LCC
    BV4596.A78 (ebook) | DDC 248.8802/47--dc23
This title was first developed as a Christian Thought and
    Process book called, Welcome to the Shivoo! (2017)

This title is dedicated to you, reader, a curious and analytical creative being, a suckling who yearns to know the true origin of your psychology and physiology;

Also, to those who nurture these creatures;

For, "Yours, O LORD, is the greatness and the power and the glory and the victory and the majesty, for all that is in the heavens and in the earth is yours. Yours is the kingdom, O LORD, and you are exalted as head above all. Both riches and honor come from you, and you rule over all. In your hand are power and might, and in your hand it is to make great and to give strength to all. And now we thank you, our God, and praise your glorious name. – 1 Chronicles 29:11–13

OTHER BISAC CLASSIFICATIONS

PSY034000 **PSYCHOLOGY** / Creative Ability
LAN002000 **LANGUAGE ARTS & DISCIPLINES** / Authorship
REL013000 **RELIGION** / Christianity / Literature & the Arts
REL067020 **RELIGION** / Christian Theology / Anthropology
REL067130 **RELIGION** / Christian Theology / Process
REL012090 **RELIGION** / Christian Life / Professional Growth

ACKNOWLEDGMENTS

Everyone in the mysterious publishing industry must start somewhere. Some work their way up from receptionist to editor. I did not ask for the job of managing partner at Capture Books, but there I found myself through a series of unlikely events, wielding that title, and operating in levels beyond my pay grade. I have wrestled.

Yet, the path on which we find ourselves, and the pockets of dirt in which we grow, are not surprising to the Creator. In fact, He probably delights in putting us into uncomfortable nests, rocked by winds too strong for us, so that we are forced to cling to Him. We, of course, may find helpers and surgical specialists in our predicaments. We did.

Many thanks belong to those I have squawked about in this book, to those who have fed worms and bugs to the nestling publisher along the way and to my creative siblings. There are so many gracious people who have offered resting places in which to reflect and to create, and there are also those who, acting like pointy sticks, forced me to rise to the edge of the nest on spindly legs for a view of the real world or tear my breast trying. These taught me to spread my wings and tip-toe over them.

These lovely souls all paint a picture of gracious creativity and tenacity in my life. An endearing friendship with the talented Debbie Nahm, helped me to grasp the meaning, struggles, and value of the creative's voice and vision in a variety of life phases. Deb embodies creativity and loyalty outside of the usual effervescence of verbal ideology. She has been a muralist, a sign painter, a furniture painter, a home stager, a doodlist, a hostess and cook for those in transition, a faux finisher, and now she is incorporating all of those stages in her Lark & Lavender farm in Colorado.

I am indebted to the fine wordsmithing of Kathy Joy, who has sent me regular notes of encouragement as she has marked through and suggested rewording of awkward phrases. In the emotional rollercoasters, I am grateful to my mother, Kathy Larkins, for her help. Tonya Jewel Blessing has also plucked and prodded me out of the nest with her questions and points of contention; I've needed Tonya as iron sharpens iron. She helped me to form a more accurate message.

Robin Bolton expertly gleaned and documented the book's footnotes and bibliography. Four eagle eyes, the savvy Chelsea Bezuidenhout, and the finishers, Crystal Schwarztkopf, Laura Padgett, and Sam Duke helped me to include more responsible things that a big picture idealist tends to overlook. Beatrice Bruno is ever the fastidious proofreader. I'm so grateful to each one.

PREFACE

Something kept tickling me. It landed delicately but kept hopping around. I couldn't swipe it away.

I swatted. Out came the juice of this book. It poured out like the spritz of a bee sting, burning under the skin of Biblical training, my much-appreciated training of God, The Image, The Person and Work of The Christ, and it stung in the void of training about the ongoing problem that God, in His humor, had made me *creative*. I had straddled the line - for decades, running my course in the conflict of mind and spirit, sweating and compromised. Unfortunately, compromise is not all it's cracked up to be.

There is a Jewish proverb that reads, "Before every person there marches an angel proclaiming, 'Behold, the image of God.'" And, what can we do with such poetry?

Articulating a theology can make for a ticklish situation in defining and quantifying one's own experience of being faithful and being a creative. I've decided to run this race in the light.

Why?

A Biblically minded creative desperately needs to understand a basis for why he or she exists as well as simply needing some practical guidelines for navigating this life.

If you were given a very valuable gift, completely unexpected, wouldn't you unwrap it, open it, be in awe, look it over and inspect it, read the warranty?

Wouldn't you ask why? Wouldn't you look at the kit instructions or the operating manual? Wouldn't you become a good steward of it — if it were a car, learn to drive, a vacation home, learn to care for the plumbing, insurance, and gardening?

As I was preparing a publisher's presentation for a homeschool conference related to our first two years in operation at Capture Books, my notes grew exponentially. Letters swept into the cloud and did not flutter down into place until after the event was over. Tragically confused, I tried to wing it.

Afterwards, I understood from the variety of encounters at that convention, that this book was sorely needed. As a publisher, I offer it to inform others about my literary concerns and what is important for authors publishing with *Capture Books*. As a Christian creative, I offer it for the long overdue discussion and debate about Biblical wisdom and ingenuity.

BEING CREATIVE offers to highlight the fact that CREATIVITY is a gift of divine proportions from the Creator, Himself.

For anyone reading this who does not understand the term, "creative", read on prayerfully and more will be revealed. One may drop into your mind or onto your doorstep providentially as you experience these chapters. Maybe you will discover a label for which you have been searching a long while.

Think of these rules as an invitation to succeed.

CONTENTS

WELCOME TO BEING CREATIVE!

WHY DOES ANYONE STRUGGLE FOR BELONGING? If the human impulse to create is a reflection of the Creator's image shaped inside of us, then why does a sense of value and purpose seem so elusive? *Maybe it's because we creatives don't quite understand our origin.*

Does a hub for creativity even exist? Isn't it up for grabs, just anyone's best guess?

The purpose of this book is to help us integrate the revelations of the triune God with our finite creativity. It is not so much a "how to write, draw, sculpt, or make films" sort of book; it is a means to think about artistry in a tradition of faithful revelation. I hope to not only articulate a sacred basis for art, but also to inspire creatives to propel themselves into their own purpose for existing. Perhaps some ideas contained in these pages will encourage the more utilitarian individual to make a proper setting—or be creative with more settings—in which to launch the excellent work of creatives and also as a means to bring them the proper honor for what is learned from their expressions.

The Creator's ingenuity is expressed in the ever-living Logos. God's speech did not flow out in a single human language because His expressions are beyond the ability of any single human tongue. He breathed anyway, and expounded His image into stories that were written in tribal languages, king's languages, and then human flesh, with expressive lips and eyes, and with abilities to interpret and understand, with dexterity of digits to articulate through touch and handling. He breathed many gifts into human blood and genes. His most clearly executed point was made in the personification of Himself, the person of Jesus, the Word in 3–D.

He continues to execute His argument for Himself in you. Yes, He breathes through YOU.

He breathed into the world a variety of organizational systems, a hierarchy of many offices of responsibility, and a purpose of bearing a bounty of spiritual fruits throughout the world. Radiant in nature, this same Ingenious Revelation also expressed His love for society through giving His laws comprised of justice and mercy.

If all of that weren't enough, when mortals damaged His Image of Earth and His Word to all on it, the expression of God personified Himself in the flesh of the Savior. As the Savior's departing gift, the Spirit of the Godhead "went live" on Earth, making all the spoken and written Word, all bodily communication that is of Him, all energy, all light and flesh to "go live" too.

Whether you consider yourself a creative, or whether you are attached to one through bloodline or through other ties or links, these ten game rules will inspire good will and good work.

The term *shivoo* is Australian lingo meaning a boisterous party. It depicts not only the sounds and tastes of imaginative processes, but it also depicts the finale of a creative celebration. A *Shivoo!*—from beginning to end— is a delectable onomatopoeia for the truest celebration. I intend for this book to be one.

The best parties and mind-bending games don't just happen. Our lives are not accidents. But, a successful celebration takes a lot of strategy, some heart, a list of resources, and a guest list. If you are interested in becoming an event organizer, you probably need someone to mimic. When you go through the event process countless times, you eventually become an expert party planner yourself. Living your best life takes some direction, nurture and practice.

Nursing a child is the most vivid image of nurturing. Yet, there are those who nurture through a variety of life's passages. Showing how to do homework, to negotiate food choices, to find better ways to socialize: all of these areas of life are nurtured by someone who knows. There are Bible colleges and seminaries for those who want to make a career of ministry, but what if scripture applies equally to nurturing musicians, artists, film-makers, crafters, and writers?

It is easy for anyone to lose their way on the winding, bumpy, intersecting paths of life without having the benefit of a central axis, so giving an axis to a creative entrepreneur is particularly important.

Creative individuals need that hub on which to spin their wheels because they have voices and images that are apt to be used, LORD willing, in public. Who do they mimic, then? Who are their mentors?

When a creative understands the rules to a game set placed on a table, he or she will begin to set up winning strategies and choose the right playing pieces.

In this game, note that there can be many varying degrees of winners because each person is being summoned to an individual path toward a unique land of stewardship. *Nevertheless, the stakes are high.*

Those who balk at the Creator's game rules may damage the gameboard and may be swept away by their errors. Those who follow them are promised rewards and blessings on earth (*See*, Psalm 37, and otherwise enumerated in this book, find God's appointment of skillful artisans to perform oversight of creating holy decor of the tabernacle. Also, Leviticus 26, Deuteronomy 30:15–20, Jeremiah 18:7–10, Proverbs 10:22, 2 Corinthians 5:10, 2 Corinthians 4:7–18, 1 Peter 3:8–9) and eventually glory (See Daniel 12:2–3, Matthew 25:12, 21 and 23, Luke 16:10–12; and 19:17–19, Romans 8:18–25, Romans 8, specifically 18–25; Ephesians 1:3–14, 1 Thessalonians 2:19–20, 1 Corinthians 9:25, Hebrews 11:6 and 13, 1 Peter 1:4–7, and 5:4, and also 2 John 1:7–8).

Enjoy the points of discussion, and make the most of your sacred and creative game.

CAPTURE BOOKS

1

"FIRST"

MEANS

PRIORITY

What does John 1:1 mean? "In the beginning was the Word and the Word was with God and the Word was God. *Nothing* exists without this Word."

Just imagine, in the beginning, God announced the news, "Hey, watch the beginning of EVERYTHING!"

"SUNRISES! SUNRISES AND SUNSETS COMING! SUMMERTIME SWIMMING IS JUST AROUND THE CORNER! WHEELS ON THE DUSTY ROAD AHEAD! FRESH PEACHES IN THE NEWS TODAY! CHERRIES, LAUGHTER! PLUMS, KISSES! TUNES, HARMONY, AND RHYTHMS! DEBATES ABOUT ENGINEERED SEEDS! STEEL AND IRON HIDDEN FOR SKYSCRAPERS! GREEN LIMES! GRASS FOR THATCH! EYES TO READ, FLIRT! EARS TO WHISPER INTO! POMEGRANATES! ROMAN NOSES! CHEDDAR AND CARAWAY!"

God announced everything with the Word of Life. Did you know that Christ was already in the beginning, *not created* by God, but being fully God, this God? Jesus, the Christ, is not only the Savior, but was this Logos Who summoned it all into existence. Colossians 1:16–18 explains that in *Christ* all things were created, things in heaven and on earth, visible and invisible, whether thrones or dominions or rulers or authorities. All things were created through Him and for Him. Christ is before all things, and in Christ, all things hold together. He is also the Head of the Church, the first to rise from the dead so that in everything, He has the preeminence in and for Life!

His most clearly executed point of argument for Himself and His message to Earth was made in the flesh, the personification of Himself, the person of—

JESUS—WHO WAS, AND IS THE LOGOS!
WATCH FOR HIM.

I can see it now: God the Father and God the Word breathed, in the beginning, which light appeared on the waft of the Holy Spirit. Three Persons, One Front, so unified that They could only be separated for one sacred purpose. And, even on that painful separation, They were agreed.

His Word didn't fall with gravity from lips as we understand lips. But lifted by the experience of creating our planetary spheres including Earth's own boundaries, He planted objects. The Word began to fill up the void with the sound and the activity of an announcement breeding results. God's own language began to shine. To find life, *ongoing life in a myriad of defining ways.*

Notes on the page began to sing their tones, their lengths, their harmonies, and together they scattered upward into the heavens, a choir.

With another word, the waters of the heavens were layered for God's purposes and they began to flow. The sea was then separated from the dry land. Animals were created—each after their kind—on another breath, another heavenly word. The seeds and leafy vegetation began to spring from the earth and curl into patterned whorls on another spiritual exhale, another word of inspiration. Then, God formed flesh. In God's image, both male and female.

I'm curious, though. How did God breathe His full expressive Self into the flesh of Christ thousands of years later? And, how did God insert the Logos into a living, written Word that lies published on a coffee table, bookshelf or on a desk seemingly inert, or in the pockets of so many? Was God's language only a verbal expression, "The Word?" Or, did it include physical energy flung like stones into a pool, some physiological forms of communication as well?

Referring to "The Word" in a Biblical sense is a mystery to Earthlings. We search our alphabet for symbols and references of connotations to the "Logos" because it is so difficult to understand the term, the God-breathed WORD.

I just love word definitions and following their connotations through. So, when I looked up the term, "word," the meaning of this verse invited me in for a deeper look.

The Word, translated, does not mean an English language noun. It does not mean the Word existed only after Gutenberg's first publishing of the Bible. It does not mean that God generated His impressions only to the left side of the human brain, which tends to control aspects of language and logic, or to the right side of the brain, which tends to handle spatial and visual comprehension.

The LOGOS, in its essential definition, means the Essential Point of Expression or Argument.[1] In this case, the Biblical author, John, uses the Logos creatively by applying it to the greatest argument for the living God, as the incarnation of God, begotten Son, superlative human, fully lit up for all to see.

"Word" is actually an incredibly cryptic translation of logos. The specific term, logos, in Greek philosophy, means "the central, defining principle or idea of an argument or philosophy." In fact, it is the hub upon which all else within the system turns![2]

So, "in the beginning," as the beginning relates to Earth, our Father God and God the Son expressed what the Godhead wanted the world to know by:

1) personally mingling, walking, and talking with those created in His image,

2) lavishing on them a perfectly-created universe and the human form with perfectly working systems, expressions, and a will to act bodily, and

3) offering a unified form of necessary imagination and communication to people: the elegant and sword-

like word of God full of history, math, law, natural science, prophecy, injunction, psychology, mercy, testimony, and justice. "Word" was the argument passed from generation to generation tucked inside image, song, drawing, story, human example, nature, and writings.

The Word then, in every other sense of creative expression, is everything else—all the bits and pieces— that God wants us to know about Himself. From the gifts of music which evoke rooted emotions without lyrics, to ever-changing projections of His hand-eye coordination in nature. From the heavens and the earth, to the comical animals and the fierce, to the fragrant and shady foliage, in diverse human abilities made in His image and imagination, and in the continuing recreation of this world's cycle of each day and night. The heavens declare the glory of God. His harvests provide food for hungry mouths, showing the Father's care. It is in the expression of God's law, ordinances, statues, poetry, drama and peace in the testimonies, stories and letters of love in the Bible, that the oil flows. All of this is God's intentional Word to us.

How safe are we as co-creators, as copycats of Christ, since He is the Head of the Church[3], since He goes before us in every creative aspect and since He also sits as the Preeminent Judge of all?[4] When I discovered this truth, my insecurities about my desires to create, the process of creating and researching whatever I was creating, the editing of what I'd created and the length of time it took to express myself properly, the space taken up in my room, the messes—I stopped apologizing. Instead, I focused on how to make everything I do, write, eat, drink, sing, love or serve, an expression of worship.[5] Artists are not necessarily lazy. We live midst the tensions of the unknown, distractions of creating, sin, and glory.

I often interrupt a creative process to answer the phone or doorbell, to do something more pragmatic, more pressing, more fun, or more financially necessary. I am a conflicted soul. Are most maker types this way? Some are more defiant in protecting their creative interests. But if someone asks me, "Whatcha doin'?" I've been known to say, "Oh, nothing. What are *you* doing?" as a means of deflecting attention away from having to explain my art, my source of reflection, my songwriting, or my poetic process.

What a weird person a creative can be!

For years, I secretly recorded music I'd written by squirreling away money and scheduling studio time when my husband wouldn't notice. He was a rocker. I was folk singer experimenting with improvisational jazz. He ducked my hints of going to concerts and festivals for dates. He desperately hoped I would not start hauling him off to bars to listen to music every weekend. I hoped to have a career somehow, someway, in some form of music making.

Of course, CDs appeared out of nowhere. After the second one, I assessed my gut instinct. Could I really see myself singing in bars or churches or maybe coffee shops? It didn't seem likely. I had become too much of a homebody. At the end of seven years and two "almost-had-a-moment" CDs, I realized the headaches in the studio were due to a variety of limitations. I also realized my duplicity.

My husband and I had an all-out battle and then a cold war about the holes in our budget and our mutual feelings of betrayal.

What I couldn't wrap my mind around at the time, was the purpose of my being created creative.

I couldn't decide what was paramount. I was all over the place.

Things are quite different now, he brags on me—to my chagrin—because he's amazed at my ongoing creativity in every phase of life; to my chagrin because, I never did anything more to develop the potential of my songs. Recording turned out to be an important means of escapism, and also therapy, to bring me through some difficult years.

I learned to be generous to others who don't share my vision. I learned to live life on life's terms between the partly swept clouds and the dust. I learned to be busy and content in the same space. I learned what a great fortune it is to be married to my adventurous and kind husband in poverty or in wealth. I learned to turn my awe of other's accomplishments into happiness for their creative paths and gifts. I learned there is a time to latch on like a catfish, and another time to let go of the ropes. I absorbed God's goodness and faithfulness like the oil of Vitamin E on a scar. I learned that the law was a world of rules and creativity unto its own – more about that later. All these things and many more were inherited from my years of musical experimentation and building houses. Sometimes a creative's road to hope and self-discovery are as important as influence and success.

What priority has God Himself put on making things?

FIRST ISN'T EVERYTHING, BUT FIRST IS PARAMOUNT.

In the beginning, God revealed Himself by creating. Apparently, this was His heart's desire. To create things, to be creative.

I see a pattern of firsts because the phrase, "In the beginning"[6] is combined with, "God created" meaning His first entrepreneurial acts.[7] These phrases are found in the first book of the Bible. *First, first, first.* The first book of the Holy Bible. First in our time (beginning), and first in God's activity on our behalf (He is First). God's Word was effectively creating (wording, speaking, breathing, expressing) light into the cosmos. And He keeps spreading understanding from the corporate office of the Godhead. God's creativity skillfully set the stage for your personal salvation.

You could argue that creating was more of necessity than priority. But an author sets the rules of His created world, and in the case of Earth, God's rationale was to create first, and the finest creativity was set into a pocket of belonging to Him. He is our Creative Hub. Knowing Him is the beginning of learning His secrets.

The Father and Holy Spirit did this with the best form of persuasion. By offering His creative subjects a place and a time, growth and purpose, with also a genetic footprint and bloodline, God gave every living thing a place to belong. God's creative joy mingled with the first humans, almost as though a writer had entered into his own plot—becoming a character in his story.

In the beginning, there was, and is, *The Being*. There was, and still is, *The Being's energetic self-expression. Creating. Persuading.* Through His artistic activity in nature, through many varied forms of communication, the revealed Logos set about welcoming human beings. He expressed *Himself* as their place of belonging. He offered this belonging to anyone in the world, for God so loved the world.[8]

WHY ARE WE IMPORTANT?

In one extraordinary move, God said, "Let's make someone like us."[9] He differentiated this living human being from His high ministering angels, from the low minerals of Earth, from all the flora and fauna, from breathing-yapping emotional animals procreating after their own kind, and from the asexual sun, moon, singing stars, and orbiting planets, by anointing the first man and woman with a measure of His own creativity. "I want family!" God declared. Hebrews 2 tells us that Jesus calls us brothers and children. He is the One Who set us apart, and the ones set apart are of the same family.

With a breath of His inspiration, humanity received layers of First Adam gifts: inspiration, imagination, the ability to love, and to learn in complexity. "Belonging" was defined as an ability to know Him personally, to be with the One who knows all things, to walk, work, and play in His gifts. Then, Christ died to redeem us from sin's domain. Creativity came prior to salvation, to evangelism, to preaching, and teaching.

The Son, Jesus, was God's creative power expressing His heart for a story and a place of belonging for all life. If you study it, the gift of creation, sin, and plan of salvation makes little sense to us. When this plan is fulfilled, it proves God's creative excellence.

In the beginning, the incomprehensible Being expressed His attributes and benefits to us via the incredible architecture of His ongoing universe. With particularity, He measured and engineered systems so that the world became a place of belonging for us.

Without God's wisdom in creation, nothing exists. Yet, this creativity is ongoing. When we work along with God's inspiration, He offers us authority for this world and into the next. We've inherited enough of His legacy, enough purposeful cunning, and His Holy Spirit to help us understand and implement the Logos together.

Understand, the Godhead always creates first in the Spirit with His Word. He creates for His own circle of joy! His creation formed and decorated a setting for us to *experience* belonging. And, a continuum.

When we express our own innovation with God's blessing, we can differentiate a new species, discover a new form of things. New combinations of ideas and skills rise to divine innuendoes under His guidance. We join with Him for contemporary or future purposes.

Focused, thinking analytically, we can understand

and implement science and physics well, write new books, design new designs, find new markets. We express more joy, broader peace, deeper concern, a purity, a true meekness, and wondrous self-confidence by accepting God's mysteries. Let's look for His ironical purposes, shall we?

- **Here's one.** Seek to become a more righteous character from day-to-day.
- **Here's another.** Exemplify sheer delight by writing around the secrets as you explore them yourself.
- **Here's yet another!** Write until intrigue infuses itself, beckoning you to spin off from the worn path, exploring the mysteries.

The Logos created the human mind to capture and direct paths of electricity, velocity, biological genes and viruses; to make engines, imagine wheels, design homes, plumbing, space shuttles. In other words, God gave us each a measure of His own creative intelligence.

Throughout the day, can you imagine bits of the Creator's glory breaking off like breadcrumbs, dropping a trail of joy in our processes, leading us on to the big Shivoo? Joy is the present assurance of the glory to come. We can sense hints of this glory in God's own feats.

The Creator often communicates through natural wonders to which adults become accustomed. It is the child who asks, *"Why, how, who, what and where?"* Adults mostly try to analyze wonders away scientifically, as if these explanations substitute for the deeper truth that God designed physics for His creative purposes.

Just listen.

When you stop using your eyes you are engaging a different part of your functioning brain, which God created for other unique purposes.

Close your eyes and consider this verse from Genesis 1:1:

> In the beginning
>
> God *created.*

Here, we have enough to contemplate a coupling.

> "In the *beginning*"
>
> and, "God created."

Two things combined to form a priority in time and in doing.

The rule of firsts is the rule of priority.

When we mimic God's creativity, we

mimic His **priority.**

SPIRITUAL THEATER VERSUS MAGIC

Magic and alchemy are both popular descriptors. Even Christians use them. Creatives can try to employ magic in a spiritual, holistic sense as though they were only metaphors or an allegory, but the practice of magic is not even close to the Biblical ideas of imagination, wonder, miracles, transformation, and illumination. Magic removes the Wonderful One from the equation of creation by mimicking true wonder with a sleight of hand.

Cutting these cords between the wonder and the Giver may feel fanciful, however, the end of this story is separation from God. An illusion can be a purposeful sleight of hand, but magic is using deception to transform, confuse, snare, and kill. Alchemy removes God's essential design.

It was only when Adam and Eve broke confidence with their Creator[10] that the wonder of God's Spirit separated from them because God is Holy and cannot mingle with sin.[11] The result was dying and death.

In love and goodness, the Lord devised another means of expression through connective blood and tissue in His covenant with us.

Imagine that God's covenant was depicted in the performance of theatrical rituals and sacrifices. Did God mean to command that His people were to engage in the theater for purposes of illumination?

Imagine, also, that community laws and festivals were meant to help those practicing gain a better understanding of His goodness and love. Imagine that they *did not* believe these edicts to be legalistic.

How did it work?

Reenacting the Lord's dramatic events kept His purposes in mind. They helped people look honestly at processing life His way. The codes and laws provided a means to treat others respectfully and compassionately.[12]

And, many of these feasts and played-out dramas were great experiences for the communities of the twelve tribes. For individuals, they gave pause for reflection. Because sin had begun to mar God's creation. But, God would implement new theatrics, special works and mighty wonders, to rescue people as He'd promised them time, and time again. Theatrics, like Moses and Aaron's feats before Pharaoh's court, were ***theatrics of grace***.

In the escape from Egypt, lifting up the walls of the Red Sea, God separated all Israel from their captors forever. Providing enough oil to get His people through an assault was a miracle during God's great silence. Bringing birds and manna to eat; later, feeding the thousands with a loaf of bread and a few fish, were all images of God's grace and lovingkindness. Preserving His own. Time and time again. The drama of Queen Esther and Mordecai saving the Jews, Daniel in the lion's den, Joseph's technicolor coat, and the dramas of David and Goliath are still favorites in the theaters of the faithful.

Christ, in the matter of creation, showed that being creative as a lifestyle is His priority. Then, He showed off His mastery of creativity by rising from the dead! Every day, He is creative. When you rise to see the colors of dawn every morning, you know this. At some point, many a child will cease to wonder and accept others' limited explanations about nature's wonders. Yet some adults continue to experience awe of nature's wonders.

In God's ongoing creativity, He contemplated rescue for any who were deaf, blind, lost, or paralyzed. He even contemplated resuscitating all those who die in Christ.[13]

Passover and Resurrection are the primary and unique colors of God's creativity. He saves souls who claim His mark, the smear of lamb's blood. The substitution of the innocent lamb's death for the penalty of our sin allows the angel of death to see our shield of protection and forces him to move along. The creative and very real story of Jesus' death and resurrection has the power to transform destruction into everlasting life.

So while God is primarily creating, rescuing, resuscitating the dead, we are co-creating, co-rescuing, co-resuscitating the dead. How is this so?

If you have been taught that winning souls is a fruit of the Spirit, check again. Winning souls is the duty of the Lord. But, we can help hand surgical tools to the Surgeon, can't we, and fertilizer to the Gardener? Let's say these represent the nine fruits of the spirit as they are listed in Galatians 5:22–23: love, joy, peace, forbearance, kindness, goodness, faithfulness, gentleness and self-control. Benedictine monks would call these spiritual practices "the conversation of life."[14]

When the father of the prophet, Sampson, was first visited by the Angel of the Lord, the father asked, "What is your name?" The angel said His name was beyond understanding, secret and wonderful. Then, while the parents were offering a sacrifice, the angel ascended in the smoke of the fire (Judges 13:17–20). Recognizing that only the Angel of the Lord could rise into the air with the smoke and disappear, the parents fell on their faces, freaked out. Wouldn't you be? The Lord's mysterious events on Earth are wonders to us because they come from the Wonderful One and from a different heaven, say, a different dimension.

It wouldn't surprise me to discover that as we are working out our own salvation in our creative and everyday lives, spiritual fruits will appear as choices. Yes, tools for God's work will appear as choices in writing themes, and in the stressors of life's interactions with others. These fruits will also aid in winning souls. So, practice drawing from the tree of life in your artistic depictions of life and in your theatrics of human relationships. Work counter-intuitively.

Theatrically, Yahweh commanded his prophet, Hosea, to marry a "wife of whoredom".[15] This Hebrew term indicates illicit sexual behavior. Moses also used the word in Genesis 38:24 to refer to Tamar's posing as a shrine prostitute in order to entice Judah to do his duty under the law by her since he had refused to give her his son in marriage, as was her God-ordained right of survival. In both cases, these theatrical acts were ordained by God for purposes that took time to unfold and to be understood. Sometimes, images are offered to creatives to use in our work. These images and tools are gifts entrusted to and for us for our good, and then as we hone and share them, they become gifts to others.

Art indeed mimics life, but art and theater can also mimic God's grace in a deep, resonating way. Hand over the good fruit to your audience, dramatic fruit connected to the Giver, the Source. Do not hand them the poison apple, the disconnected magical fruit.

EXAMPLES OF GOD'S THEATRICAL FIRSTS

1.   **God *must* create before any of His other plans** take hold, according to His own ordinances. As a plan, salvation was, and is, the evidence of God's creativity. We have to assume that the Lord enjoys being creative just because it is His nature. The details of God's law, the written word, and fleshing out the Christ, came much later in human history and in God's revelation, after "in the beginning God created."

2.   **Giving back the first crop.** There is another treasure hidden in the theme of the first fruits. It is the story of honor and dependance.

What does it mean to have the first fruit crop and to actually give it back to God, the first fruits of your labor? Imagine a seed germinating underground in the winter and then springing to life with the first buds of summer, becoming fruit. Is this some kind of cruel joke? Are we the peasants and Christ, a medieval lord of the manor?

Giving our first fruits creates an image of personal absolute reliance in the goodness of the Creator, that He will supply all you need.

Additionally, this reliance is a form of giving deference and honor. It is a model of how to weave life together within His community of faith. He indicates this tithe is for sharing with the community depending upon His care, and for charity.

3. **The significance of the first child.** What does it mean in priority, to have a first child? We know that in Biblical history the first child obtained the first and best, most complete blessing. The first male was dedicated to God because God claimed him.[16] He was destined to assume the role of family leader, given authority, double inheritance, and special rights. The Law forbade the disinheriting of the firstborn.[17] The first animal to breach the womb was to be sacrificed to God or redeemed by an offering.[18]

When God reached over the first to bless the second child, He was making quite a scene. Putting the second first, made news several times over in scripture. Jacob and Esau experienced it.[19] Jacob later reenacted the experience with Ephraim and Manasseh.[20] Reuben's right as the firstborn of Jacob was taken away because of sin.[21] When God made the earth, giving creative-mimicking powers to the first man and woman, He signified a right, rule, and inheritance over the animals and plants and other created things. Yet, in Colossians 1, Paul uses the word, "preeminent" to express the position of Christ in relationship to all things in heaven and on Earth. Christ was the second Adam.

Jesus, the Second Adam, displaced our assumption of ourselves being front and center. He has all rights to everything. These instances are recorded because of the theatrical anomaly: the rule of firsts was broken.

"The Word," *personally* refers to the Son of God come as the incarnation of the Father, taking on baby flesh comprised of honor and glory as humanity beheld Him full of grace and truth. Our most specific right, rule, and inheritance is found in Emmanuel. Not only is He LORD, but He is also our dramatic well to drink from, and our dramatic pattern. Believers are foreordained to be conformed to His image as we draw close to Him and allow His Spirit to infuse our spirits with His life, His ideas, and His authority.[22]

This Word of flesh creatively clothed Himself in humility, even washing the dirty feet of His followers. Do you see the theatrical character arc? Now the first becomes last. The Prince becomes the menial servant.

Christ obeyed His unique purpose to redeem us not by trading places to become our servant, but by lowering Himself more, to accept the place of a murderous, thieving criminal. Taking the punishment of a criminal, dying a torturous death, He bought us back. He paid every debt we owed to God. His change of places reconciled us with our Maker.

He imagined, ordained, and accepted His own drama on the cross for the joy that was set before Him. Separated from God the Father in death, He was raised again in triumph. Jesus is the *dramatic* first fruit of the resurrection from the dead in this drama of blood and life,[23] and many will follow Him in the twinkling of an eye.[24] Why should we not allow our own personal dramas to play out? Why not stage dramas for viewers? How many more stories can be gleaned from the stories of preeminence and patterns of firsts?

4.   **Primarily, Gifts are for the Community of Believers.** God's gifts are more than benefits. Both spiritual and physical giftedness from God are reflections of the Giver's heart for you and me. If you take note of the treasures you find walking with Him, you see these to be God's personal embraces of you. And, through you, His gifts may offer some primary nutrition for the community of faith. Maybe also your gifts and talents will become opportunities for strangers and foreigners outside the family of faith. The Father does treat His family specially well. We can trust Him to protect and provide for us. Isn't this provision in itself a witness and testimony to others and a means of wooing them to the kingdom? Our cups should spill over.

> Is being creative our sole aim?
> If not, what is the aim of being creative?

UTTER DEPENDENCE

The first thing we understand as creatives and makers is that we are utterly dependent on something or Someone higher in power and creativity than ourselves. If we breathe in and breathe out with intention and cognizance, we can suddenly experience this human dependence on a Giver of Life and breath and health.

Consider expression as an abundance of physical acts of the will and of our unconscious behaviors e.g., facial expressions that escape the body with or without words. Adam received the first body with fingers to wield tools to put inspiration into existence, to create things. Without a physical body, how would all this godlike inspiration find a use, an expression, or an outlet?

There are a myriad of expressions in the Logos to draw from. Wine makers understand they are completely interactive and dependent upon the weather and soil.

Much of your own creative success lies beneath the surface until it begins to resonate with what others are thinking and feeling. Comedians find their talent because they discover that others find them funny. It is a gift. So, in the beginning, God's gift is your raw material. What you pull together and release into the world will make for a fine tribute to God as it helps others.

Anglican Bishop N.T. Wright offers the idea that if a set of actors faithfully followed a director, a script, and the stage direction to act out four scenes of a written play, they could also be trusted to faithfully improvise a fifth act.[25] *Memorizing the details, understanding the writer's theme, and embodying the director's flow of this story would be critical to pulling off an improvised fifth act, wouldn't it? What fifth act is God calling you to improvise in your life today? Can you safely move onto the stage, face the other actors, and fill the theater with a visual and verbal embodiment of grace or mercy?*

Your creativity, at first, is not often the finest expression. It shows spirit, but may lack gloss, detail, proofreading or testing. The hook, the skill, the expert choice of the right material may be missing. The performance style may need direction, and sometimes your work even lacks the proper context. Some things are invented before their time, and because they are out of pocket, people don't recognize the significance of what has been created. This, too, is a gift.

Leonardo da Vinci created many mechanical tools and systems because people needed them. On the sly, Leonardo's God-given creativity caused him to experiment with medicine and cadavers. He was looking into things banned as unorthodox at the time, but which later were proven to be medical breakthroughs.[26]

As a creative, do you ever find yourself confused about how to prioritize your interests and activities? Do you feel like a jar of river water all shaken up, unable to determine what's most important? Sometimes, just processing through the things that interest us begins to help us understand what is important. Learning the nature of things takes time as water separates from silt.

In her book, *Plain and Simple: A Woman's Journey to the Amish*, Sue Bender wrote, "I never thought to stop and ask myself, 'What really matters?' Instead, I gave everything equal weight. I had no way to select what was important and what was not. Things that were important didn't get done, and others, quite unimportant, were completed and crossed off the list."[27]

Sue was referring to her habits of keeping her house clean, grading papers, and visiting friends, and to her desire to produce art that was special so that she would be thought of as special. "Accumulating choices was a way of not having to make a choice, but I didn't know it at the time. To eliminate anything was a foreign concept. I felt deprived if I let go of any choices."[28]

As we consider the meaning and value of things, the King of Creation orchestrates the events of life. Occasionally, He lets us in on His secrets. As we write or produce art, He'll help us process it for His purposes.

BEING CUNNING WITH RAW MATERIALS

We don't really create in a void, but sometimes it feels like we're tasked with creating something from nothing.

Creating in a personal void is really creating with the raw materials given by the Heavenly Father, both the acid and the sweetness in a life, and the opportunities given by the Great Designer. As a child is utterly dependent upon his or her parent for the raw materials of life, and for some directives and guidance, so a Creative is dependent on the Creator's supply and purposes. If He stops everything, that's it. If He opens an avenue, a journey, and favor in a direction, that is the direction we will most assuredly take and find purpose.

Jesus went to the desert to be alone with His Father God for 40 days.[29] Moses ran from Pharaoh into the desert where he stayed for the rest of his life as a nomad.[30] Not all who wander are lost. Jesus became so full of His experience with His Father that when Satan came to tempt Him, Jesus' retorted, "I have food you know nothing of."[31] When Moses left all of the riches, authority, and the attachments of his stepmother and her royal household behind, he found his exquisite wife and became the leader whom God intended for him to become.[32] All this came to being through communion with God. To find meekness through self-examination as Moses did, or strength to face all the temptations of life as Jesus did, consider the solace of the Father's company alone when you need direction.

Creativity is, *in essence,* being "cunning." This word has taken on a sour connotation, as has the word "creative," but Biblically, cunning is only defined in the positive sense. It means being ingenious, gifted with finesse, wise.[33] Yet, if you set something newly created before an audience, it might not appear *all that* cunning. You might get a stunned look, a jail sentence, or nervous laughter for reward. Being a creative person requires that you continue to focus on the standards of the craft to improve.

Standards belong to the Lord. Ideas, lyrics, melodies, and fairy tales improve their purpose and communication with honing, with accountability and with renewed teamwork. New renderings and settings often improve upon the original. But, we have to accept the gift in its original form first.

People try to quantify what Christian books or Christian art is. Some people require the name of Jesus to be announced like a seal of "Christian" work. Some require a clear narrative of the cross and resurrection of Christ in every story. But, if this were the only aspect to a godly life, only the book of John would exist in scripture. Do you know, all good ideas, all good results from hard research, all good inspiration, are by the Creator's hand. He often gives His inspiration and anointing to those who do not even recognize Him at work? In fact, there is so much more to absorb through nature, through what the various books of the Bible teach us, and through what the Holy Spirit invites us to.

Our creative expressions should aim to be true to nature as God designed it. Labels are judgments that only God can determine.

Everybody serves God's purposes. God uses whom He uses for different purposes. His purposes are above ours. Still, I would rather be a friend of God, a beloved of the Creator, than a mere servant. Wouldn't you?

I hope you understand that you, personally, are of high priority. "For this reason, since the day we heard about you, we have not stopped praying for you. We continually ask God to fill you with the knowledge of his will through all the wisdom and understanding that the Spirit gives, so that you may live a life worthy of the Lord and please him in every way: bearing fruit in every good work, growing in the knowledge of God."[34]

Rule 1: ACCEPT THE GIFT. Let your body and mind marinate in this wonder, this awesome gift of being creative. Imagine His creativity seeping into each part of your body.

From the International Standard Bible Encyclopedia, W.L. Walker explains the biblical use of the term "cunning:"

"kun'-ing (chakham, chashabh): In Bible-English "cunning" means always "wise" or "skilful"; the word does not occur in the bad sense, and it is found in the Old Testament only. The chief Hebrew words are chakham, "wise," "skilful" (2 Chronicles 2:7 the KJV "a man cunning to work in gold"; 2 Chronicles 2:13 Isaiah 3:3 the KJV, etc.); chashabh, "to think," "devise," "desire" (Exodus 26:1, 31; Exodus 28:6 and 15 the KJV, etc.). We have also da`ath, "knowledge" (1 Kings 7:14 the KJV); bin, "to be intelligent" ( Chronicles 25:7 the KJV); machasbebheth, "thought," "device," "design" (Exodus 31:4; Exodus 35:33, 15 the KJV); 'aman, "artificer" (Songs 7:1 the KJV); yadha` "to know," once translated "cunning" (Daniel 1:4 the KJV). For cunning the ASRV gives skilful" (Exodus 31:4, etc.; Isaiah 3:3 "expert"); for "cunning work" the work of the "skilful workman" (Exodus 26:1, 31, etc. the ERV "cunning workman"); for "curious," "skilfully woven," the ERV "cunningly woven" (Exodus 28:8, etc.)."

2

ACKNOWLEDGE
THE CREATOR

To acknowledge means to recognize, to credit, to put what you know on a platform. It's right in the word.

If we are honest with ourselves, we'll admit that we don't know where our best ideas come from. They are given to us through a series of ideas and events. Sometimes we solve problems in our sleep. Sometimes, we wake up with the lyrics to a song, or a twist in a story. God helps us create even while we are unconscious. Psalm 16:7 says, "I will praise the LORD, who counsels me; even at night my heart instructs me."

When you are in awe of a scent, a flavor, a life, a single act of kindness, give thanks.

A child can be taught to say "thank you", but for a child to experience gratitude, he or she must experience a sense of wonder or meekness. It is the same for adults.

If creativity is a gift, there is a source. The gift did not magically appear out of nowhere.

The gift has a giver. There is a source.

If ingenuity comes to you as a lark, let some tremulous harmonies flow from your heart for a blessing. Experience goodwill in tasting a flavor. You've been blessed for purposes unknown. Give thanks.

- "Thank you, God, that in the beginning, and ongoing, all creation sprouts from Your Good Character."

- "Thank you, God, for occasionally putting me into a corner to think through details, temperature, space, time, and physics."

- "Thank You, God, for the fat, the herbs, and the spices I can eat, making things good."

- "Thank You for the sigh of relief in going to the bathroom."

- "Thank You, God, for painting the clouds in prisms at day's beginning and day's ending."

- "Thank You, Lord, for Psalms, for thoughtful secular music, and spiritual songs to sing. Thank you, that when I sing, something unique changes in my brain function."

- "Thank You, God, for language and cultural accents, codes, secrets, and revelations.

- "Thank You for gender, sexuality, and sensual communication."

- "Thank You for the organization of time."

- "Thank You, for helping me create a legacy."

- "Thank You, for making me work with those who humor me and those who compel me."

- "Thank You, God, for inviting me to work with both sides of my brain, and with the gray matter as well as the white matter."

Jot down something that occurred to you in gratitude. For, this is the proverb for beginning a journey in wise creativity: "In all your ways acknowledge Him, and He shall direct your paths, making the rough places smooth and the crooked straight."[1] Creativity begins with a sense of awe, and meekness. It leads to gratitude, authenticity and hope.

A comedic story by Jon Courson was published in *Searchlight*. Attributing credit to whom credit is due can be a blind spot. "An elephant and a flea walked over a creaky wooden bridge. When they reached the other side, the flea said to the elephant, 'Wow! We sure made that bridge shake, didn't we?'"[2]

"Trusting the LORD with all your heart,
Not putting confidence in your own understanding, in all your ways acknowledging Him, by recognizing His character is at work and at play, so that you can have the confidence to work, walk or dance in faith. Walking with Him, submit to Him, and
He will direct your path."
Proverbs 3:5–6

Creating great work, being cunning and skillful, always starts with an dedication, ultimately to the Creator.

"Whatever you do, whether in word or deed,
do it in the name of the LORD Jesus Christ,
giving thanks to God and the Father by Him."
Colossians 3:17

ACKNOWLEDGING GOD IN PRAISE AND WORSHIP

Praise and worship are two different attitudes often used in the same phrase as though they are one and the same. The inspiration which comes to us while in praise and worship is channeled from two different psychologies.

Praise rises above mundane inertia from where we find ourselves; it moves upwards in accolades. "Praise" is not a *genre of music*; rather, praise is any communication that sincerely acknowledges and describes attributes due to another. We use praise to articulate the ways in which God is elevated over all. Praise exalts the one worthy of it with, or without, song. Praise includes the idea, "I can do this because YOU can do this."—directed at God's abilities. It is primarily vertical.

Praise becomes more exciting when words extolling someone's attributes are woven together with visual images. Add music to be experienced through the sensory system to invoke a complex set of emotions. Watch as new waves of thinking evolve. See, cognitive thinking and involuntary experience complement each other in order to comprise a beautiful marriage.

Words along can leave your compliment to someone just shy of the desired response. Sometimes simplicity works, but at times, a verbal compliment absent a gift may not express the depth of your tribute.

When you add emotional images, a personal gift, a scent, musical harmonies and rhythms, a real tribute is shown of your efforts to praise the one you admire.

Worship has the aspect of physiological bowing, of meekness, of humbly prostrating one's body before God. Romans 12:1–2 makes it clear that our reasonable and true sacrifice of worship involves our full body submission on a daily basis to the LORD. Does your experience with church and with the LORDship of Christ bring you to your knees or to your stomach, face on the ground at times? Perhaps this is hyperbole, but maybe we could try worshiping by this recommendation in order to acknowledge the correct relationship we have in meekness to God. Worship can be expressed musically and thoughtfully, in contemplation. But is contemplation a full body response? Contemplation is a meditation on a subject perhaps with some analysis.

Worship is acknowledging that "In the beginning God created the heavens and the earth." (Gen. 1:1) We understand this singular declaration denotes the vast difference between God's ability to create from scratch and our ability to mimic His creativeness in our lifetimes because we are created in His image. Worship is a laying of our lives before His feet and praying that He be the One to raise us up when, and how, He chooses.

Worship extends to our daily work and play, our interactions with others and to charitable work in acknowledgement of the One Who Rescues. With or without contemplation, worship is the correct posture of a believer's heart to the LORD in waking hours, in all endeavors, in work, contemplation, or play.

Does it follow then, when we experience creativity flowing through us, this "flow of consciousness" a mystery often taken for granted, should be understood to be God's invisible qualities pouring out of our created beings?

Is this voice to affect new creations?

Maybe. Our efforts display His own eternal power and divine nature as our cups run over.

Here it is: "For since the creation of the world God's invisible qualities—His eternal power and divine nature—have been clearly seen, being understood from what has been made, so that people are without excuse." Let's unpeel the layers. What does the Romans 1:20 statement about creation mean?

Does it appear to say that since the beginning of the world God's creativity is a testimony or reflection of two invisible qualities, those being

a) His eternal power and

b) His divine nature?

It seems, because of His ongoing creativity in this world, we experience many proofs of both: His power and divinity.

It also seems to say that everyone can clearly see, and we understand from what has been made and is being made today. These qualities of God's eternal power and divine nature provide tangible evidence.

This statement lays it down plainly that people are without excuse to deny these attributes of God the Creator when the display of His acts are clearly understood to be tangent mirrors of His glory.

We are standing with open hands.

THE ODD SURPRISES OF GOD

All the works of God are marvelous, and though I should know that full well—theoretically—I might take for granted the variety of God's work in my day-to-day experience.

Would you smash a moth or butterfly for landing on your arm?

Would you smash it if it were blue or maybe orange or brown?

If instead, it landed on your chest creating an uneasy flutter, would you take up the fly-swatter?

I've seen fresh-faced flocks from their cocoons swarming a rose bush in spring, a tall bush shuddering like prisms of heaven, queerly afire but not consumed.

I saw a loveliness of ladybugs, too. A frightening horde of them, swarming on wood.

An undulating blanket of red on rotting logs, feasting like termites, is this how they're born?

Never before had I seen more than one or two of the bugs land at a time, playful, and favored, a sense of delight.

But this fleet of wings swarming the surface, frightened my senses; intrigued me in purpose.

And, in the profundity, for God in His odd act, I stepped back, I stepped back.

Life, fresh-faced, in singles, in swarms, talked back to the control I perceived was the form. A blessing of life, a favor, a strike, and who would I be to smash the surprise?

Another example, the ever-changing skies from dawn to the next dawn, day after day, are full of physics and wonder. My scientific friend says it's just the amount of water in the prisms of air. It's the combination of chemicals mingling with temperature. All true, yet I can't help but wonder why Our Creator is the only One who can put on such displays around the world, morning and evening. Our seasons, our blood moons, our winters, our hurricanes, our desert floods all display the awesome Creator acts, something good, something terrifying in friction and surprise.

The LORD deserves our gratitude and public tribute for granting us a part in His mysterious glory.

Bubbling laughter and rivers of deep joy are as profound as enjoying some fresh, cold water. These are easy to see as beneficial works of God. There are many benefits that can come even from famine, digging for water, lament, tragedy, illness, loss, and sacrifice.

To omit darkness and uncertainty in this life as beyond the realm of a divine gift, is to omit our own response and analysis, the reality and truth, the help received from comforting people, and the purpose of redemptive powers.

When we experience these frustrated times, times when our aims are thwarted, we can learn that God's gifts prove better and more purposeful than our own ideals. We face the cycle of life and death. We have time to reflect and reorganize priorities, and we often grow closer to God when we are the most confused.

Being Creative

If not the fondest affection, then beauty.
The face of a toddler, a loopy discussion,
Lily ponds in bloom and refreshing,
Swaths of sky rising in a sun's setting.
If never a human bends to my longing,
Give me the golden drapes of willows
And grasses in fields, dancing in billows.
Let there be silence and cadence, mysterious
Music seeping through serious liturgy
Reaching orphans and widows of poetry,
Flights of fireflies darting through forests,
If not the tender lover be sworn.
Bring me horns of cicadas and peepers,
The muse of barbecues, sweet peas, and roses,
Perfuming bouquets and pillows of lilies,
Games to play after soup and brioches.
If not the fondest affection, then beauty.
Give me a snow-dusting swirling in sheers,
Eyelet curtains of snow branches pierced,
Warming and blue and combed-cotton mists
And songs like the sea surfing on what it sifts.
Helpfulness, bring me, and storms of glee.
All of this, surely is air to breathe
Sweetly Your promise, a lengthy bequest,
An inner reverb that Your eye holds me fast.
If lovers will fail me, a walk and a talk,
You clasp my heart's key, insert, unlock.

CHARADES AS GIVER

Some would argue that God is not always the Creator, that there is another creator who prowls around like a roaring lion. This evil one may indeed charade as the Creator, but he is not a Creator in the upper case. Creator is defined as One Who is Able to make something from nothing. Our own creativity at best is able to make something from very little.

My editor, Victoria Pless, wrote in the margin of this manuscript, "The problem, as I see it, is even a Christian could then attribute the sinful things to God if they/we are not careful." It's true. How many artists, writers, and musicians have said, "The LORD told me to–"? Yet, if inspiration is absent, or the facts, or the truth, or if excellence or integrity is absent, I wonder whether they've finished the task regarding their calling.

In order to manicure the lawn, the debris must be picked up, and the lawn mown and edged. As I was going about with the pooper-scooper-upper, dodging the hidden feces in the leaves and shadows, I saw a correlation to sin. Sin often hides in the middle of beauty and goodness. God did not come to forgive sin. God came to forgive the sinner. Because Jesus paid sin's penalty,[3] the sinner is forgiven, and the sin is separated from him or her. But sin itself is never forgiven or allowed to co-exist with God.[4]

I scooped up the dog poo and the lurking wild rabbit, squirrel, and bird droppings, too, thinking how often writers and makers avoid calling out mistakes and sins against God supposing that we aren't supposed to be offensive. We worry, perhaps, about sales. Sometimes artists create mentally unhinged things. Perversions of logic and beauty stand to show us the difference between true and clever inspiration, and a lack thereof. God cannot even look at sin.[5] He separates us from our sin as far as the east is from the west.[6] Holy God does not make deals with the devil—in art, this would be perverse. *Neither do we.* If we design an evil situation in a story or a perverse character, our aim is to speak truth and wisdom even there. The perversity is when a writer or creator might lead an audience to desire or become enslaved to that which is cursed by God.

In our creations, we need to be tender-hearted toward our characters but depict an eye-opening event or a sin-surgeon to surgically remove the sin. This spotlight moment or harsh eradication of evil from a character, serves to depict a) God's glory and b) the reader's wonder about how transformation occurs.

The evil one masquerades as Creator. His aim is not a good, loving, or transformative one. He is an imposter. His aim is to deceive, steal, kill, and destroy.[7] In that case, the writer or producer needs to suggest a clear message about where that choice leads.

The LORD's purpose is to give us a full, rich, and satisfying life.[8] In the beginning, God created, yes, but because of Love's gift of free will to us, sin entered the world.[9] Because of Satan's pride in wanting to be like God, he was thrown out of heaven and now roams the earth.[10] God is not the author of sin or sinful actions. He is Creator and Redeemer. What a shame to begin serving the Creator, yet in the end, find you are serving the devil! The apostle warned, "Be sober-minded and alert. Your adversary the devil prowls around like a roaring lion, seeking someone to devour. Resist him, standing firm in your faith and in the knowledge that your brother and sisters throughout the world are undergoing the same kinds of suffering."[11]

Bob Dylan's lyric said it clearly: "Ya gotta serve somebody. It may be the devil, an' it may be the LORD, but ya gotta serve somebody."[12]

When Jerusalem stumbled and Judah fell, it was because all of their expressions were against the LORD. They rebelled against His glorious presence.[13] As partakers in His glory, we should not aim to operate along the edge of the cliff, mixing with temptations. Recognizing the shallows helps us wade into deeper maturity and to enjoy full glory. Learn to recognize and credit the good to the Giver and the bad to the Imposter.

Look at the fruits of a creative work. If it provokes depression or suicide, it does not fall within a Christian's definition of true creativity. It is rather a trick, a gimmick, or the indulgence of a thief. "For although they knew God, *they did not honor Him as God or give thanks to Him,* but they became futile in their thinking, and their foolish hearts were darkened."[14]

Creatives can feel god-like in their creative experiences because they actually are created in God's image. They are participating in His creative personality when they work out an inspiration to a full quality.

Parents often have to instruct little children to say thank you, but it is only when they feel a sense of awe, wonder, or meekness that they can feel truly grateful. How often do we forget to return thanks to our Creator ourselves? Is it because we feel no awe at His blessings?

"When God made the heavens and the earth," Bob Deffinbaugh explained, "He created Adam and Eve in His image. They were to reflect God's image and His glory by ruling over creation. Satan tempted them to reach for a greater glory, the glory of being like God (see Genesis 3:5). When they followed Satan and disobeyed God, Adam and Eve fell, and all mankind fell with them (Romans 5:12–21).
Satan was a magnificent being with a splendor second only to His Creator. But his reflected, secondary glory was not enough for him. He wanted more. He wanted God's glory (Isaiah 14:12–14). Because of his greed for God's own glory, Satan fell. All history is evidence of his continuing effort to tempt men to pursue a 'God-like glory,' not by trusting in God but by striving to be like God."[15]

Don't be deceived, my dear brothers and sisters. "*Every* good gift and *every* perfect gift is from above, coming down from the Father of lights with whom there is no variation or shadow due to change."[16] *It is one thing to feel glad and thankful, it is another to express personal gratitude to the Giver.* So, return thanks to God for being able to participate in His creative expressions, for being gifted with a measure of His own creativity. Ephesians 2:10–11 exposes this destiny. For we are God's workmanship, *created in Christ Jesus* to do good works, which God prepared in advance as our way of life (BSB). We are meant to create GOOD works.

God is an artist. The Supreme Artist. When we appreciate God's strong arm and His transcendence, His wonders performed, we may still, even then, forget to thank God directly for them. We may forget to give Him tribute in His rightful place and for His loving intent toward us.

Remember? Creativity is the sense of awe, wonder and meekness leading to acts of hope, gratefulness and authenticity.

Does the Great Architect stop designing sunrises or sunsets or stop making trees quake or give shade in summer when people ignore His work? If we forget to acknowledge Him or refuse to honor Him, will He forget us? Or because you shake a fist in the air rather than tithing to charity, does He turn off the lights in the sky?

So long as we are on Earth, the Giver keeps giving nutrients, infusions of grace, warnings, and meaning because God loves creating.

On the next page, *sing* Psalm 1 to the traditional hymn tune: THIS IS MY FATHER'S WORLD.[17]

Psalm 1 is a tutorial piece primarily aimed to hook the spirit and will of a person into the wisdom of walking with God's counsel.

PSALM 1

You'll be safely on your way
To avoid the scoffer's play;
The counsel of ungodly minds
Leads only to dismay
Oh, learn to love God's law!
Recall it day and night;
You'll prosper as you walk with God,
Enjoying what is right.

Like a little tree will thrive
Planted by the water's side,
In season it will yield its fruit,
How green its leaves abide!
See how these roots take hold,
Set against the roots that fail,
Swept up like chaff upon the wind,
The withered roots shall sail.

Defenseless in God's court,
The lawless cannot stand;
God's righteous hand will cast them out,
Their ruin close at hand.
The One, He is our God!
He cares for large and small.
The good intent, the provident,
He shall establish all.[18]

Can you feel your toes reaching like tree roots into the splashing nearby stream? Are you soaking up the river? Will this new drink produce new fruit?

Because He is a God of hope, He provides new opportunities for characters dying to be transplanted, dying to be re-rooted, used, or transformed. Redeeming and procuring a realigned purpose is His aim. He peels back the old and gives new life. An example of this story trajectory, Jesus gave new names to His disciples as He exchanged the old giving them a new stream.

Is it easier to do daily tasks with a song in your heart? Does a grateful song open up some problem-solving abilities you wouldn't otherwise have? I wonder what would happen if we tried singing the Psalms in our Bible studies and fellowship groups. Singing thanksgivings.

The following scripture, Colossians 3:15–17, like the wheels on a bicycle work in tandem, calls us to sing and then *do* creative activities, not just contemplate them.

Let the peace that Christ gives control your thinking. It is for peace that you were chosen to be together in one body. And always be thankful. Let the teaching of Christ live inside you richly. Use all wisdom to teach and counsel each other. Sing psalms, hymns, and spiritual songs with thankfulness in your hearts to God. Everything you say and everything you do should be done for Jesus your LORD. And in all you do, give thanks to God the Father through Jesus.

Rule 2: AWE & GRATEFULNESS. BREATHE IN. ALLOW TIME AND SPACE FOR WONDER. Consider the value of the Creator's gifts to you. BREATHE OUT. Imagine offering each part of your body to Him. Determine to bring Him tribute from the first fruit.

TO TRANSFORM

A bed of iris rhizomes taught me something about the Creator's winnowing tactics. I had left the irises all spring and summer. They became infiltrated with grass.

It seemed daunting to try to pull out the grass that year. Every time I yanked at a few long pieces in irritation, the situation hollered, "I need your focused attention, please!" So, in the fall, I decided to pull out all those evil pencil grasses choking my prized spring flower bed.

It was difficult work digging up the entire bed and chopping apart the clumps of rhizomes and wrestling them from the clinging earth.

Hidden within each clump were mimicking grass roots that clung to the rhizomes as if they were the stabilizing hairs of the rhizomes. The grass roots, though they looked succulent and almost identical to the hairs of the root, were not part of the root at all. They didn't belong, they were fakers. They would never produce blossoms for me. How could I tell?

When I tugged at each hair of the rhizome, they clung to the root because they belonged. When I tugged at a grass root, it would slide out of the other hairs, because it was not connected by anything other than dirt.

This hard work made me think about the work that the Lord does in pulling out the wild grasses in my life. This work must be done even in the lives of mature individuals and colorful groups of people.

Even healthy, good grass is just "weedy" when woven into beds of blooming irises.

Learning to thank the Gardener of our souls for the means in which He manhandles our lives will help us recognize that it is for our good, in order to keep us healthy and blooming.

There's a recurring nightmare, no, a memory, that has haunted me more and more as I become older and older. It is the story of doing my part-time job of being a traveling home health care worker. I did it while finishing my last year of college and also to support my Christian Artists Network Service which comprised the bulk of my after-school time allotted to collecting contacts for musicians, youth groups, coffee houses, and church contacts, holding board meetings, setting up networking meetings, interviewing bands and band musicians, hiring journalists of the arts and writers, artists, and promoters. I also formatted the monthly newspaper.

I was hired by the home healthcare service to go to a couple of private homes in the morning, spend an hour interviewing the client, cleaning their kitchen, making them a meal, and reporting back to the supervisor. This was in the days before mobile phones. Car phones were a thing, but only realtors and other business people installed them.

One morning, I went into a woman's home who had returned from the hospital after a debilitating stroke. She could not speak or tell me what she wanted. She sat in a wheelchair already dressed for the day in a typical cotton housedress, with her nylons pulled up and her shoes tied, but her eyes were rimmed red and she stared with what seemed like desperation into my face. Her eyes pooled with tears.

On the couch was a lanky young man who was said to be her grandson. I was told that he was staying with his grandma to help her during her recovery. There was something wrong with him. He wound up his lower appendages into the air in a cross-legged position, and he picked his toenails as he leaned back into the corner of the couch and giggled.

The whole scene unnerved me. I kept asking what was wrong. First, I asked the woman who could not say. Her tears spilled down her hot cheeks. I asked the young man who rocked and giggled and picked his toenails. I touched the woman's limbs and body and head asking, 'Is it here? Is it here?" No answer. "Can I take you to the bathroom? Do you need to go?" No answer.

I quickly washed up her dishes and told her that I would have a supervisor come check on her. It took me an hour to drive back to the agency, make the report and then wait for an appointment with the supervisor who was in a meeting with someone else.

Remembering that situation has startled me awake from a deep sleep several times lately. Sometimes it comes as I am trying to go to sleep. Sometimes, I think about it as I imagine the punishments to come in my own old age. Was there something more I could have done? Was that young man abusing his grandmother? Was he just irritating her to death? Were her nylons cutting off her circulation or stuck into crevices cutting her? Should I have laid her on the bed and undressed her to take a look? Why did the family feel the need to put her in nylons anyway? Were her shoes laced too tight? Did she have a rash?

My heart begins to pound. Sometimes I cry.

As a young woman in college, I had no inkling about the sufferings of old age. I remember putting that house on someone else's list because I knew handling it was over my head. The memory of it was shoved into a container at the back of my mind, and there it stayed until this past year. Could I have been more creative in finding answers and making sure the woman found peace?

This kind of experience is fodder for a writer, don't you think? Why do I run from it? The pain of admitting it here is tell-tale. I've never spoken about it to anyone. Guilt or false guilt, it tracks me down. I'm sure Satan is alive and well because of this story I carry around.

Everyone has these stories. They say that as you get

older, your more recent memories fade, but the memories of your youth shine like the sun, and you can retell them to others with vivid detail. God, have mercy.

The things we can never quite understand are the stories that need to be told because these are the stories of life that make us yearn for heaven and wholeness, and the lifting of the veil, the healing.

These stories are what motivate us to make life better for those who follow us. They motivate us to be more creative. Can we train better, create better systems? Someone may never disclose the secret for their passion but it will creatively motivate them in a myriad of ways. Even times of horror can offer us a path to redemption.

Creativity is not an end in itself, but it is a worthy path to the primary aim of doing better in our world and bringing glory to our Maker.

Living an honest, yet creative life is the closest sort of metaphor to living a life of faith in the kindness of God's grace that I can think of.

Music infuses grace as a spirit-transforming wonder like other spiritual blessings. In faith and in creativity, there are many risks. Yet there is hope!

Inspiration? Many adjustments are needed to hone it into something new and creative. So many prayers are lifted. God is involved and intervenes.

Being creative in a godly sense means accepting the gift of inspiration in the layers of life and turning out something of positive purpose from very little. Like —

- You give someone scissors and cloth, and a costume is made.
- You give legs and feet to a baby, and the babe usually takes a step forward.
- You give someone a disaster, and find a human pulling a wagon with a child in it.
- You put a few orphans with ingenuity on a trash heap in South America or Africa, and they make violins, drums, and flutes out of the rubbish, and play music.
- You give someone a maniac, and they put a history onto her like a sack of stones so that you find the salt of sympathetic tears, weeping empathy, dashed upon her oily hair. You learn God's mercy, and maybe God's redemption. For, learning to experience mercy can be an artistic leap.
- An author begins to tuck together musical education, a Bible degree, and poetic experience into the discipline of setting the Biblical Psalms into singable *Psalm Hymns.* This is done while enduring the slander and libel of neighbors and defending against malicious criminal accusations in court.

James J. Davis, a Welsh miner who became the secretary of labor two years after the Pennsylvania anthracite mine disaster of June 5, 1919, wrote, "I think the reason I have never cared for drink is this: the ease from mental pain that other men have sought in alcohol, I have always found in song." All the men of the Orpheus Glee Club were survivors, sons or brothers of miners who left their jobs after the disaster and began to sing. Davis went on to reflect, "The whole land of Wales echoes with the folk songs of a people who sing because they must."[1]

Often, transformation will sneak in through the back door with a tug of emotion. Best-selling author Philip Yancey grew up hearing conflicting messages preached about God. Eventually, he turned his back on religion. God eventually wooed him with art into becoming a transformative storyteller himself. He attributes neither the Bible nor preaching to his real, mindful conversion to Christianity, but rather to three elements of God's creativity: the fierce beauty of nature, musical classics, and romantic love.[2]

There are times when the use of creativity alone forms the question a soul needs for transformation. An idea can convince by personal communication and understanding without a word of teaching. A gentle turning of the head is won by opening a blinder.

Once upon a time, a mother and daughter were standing in a line at a fair, waiting to go on a ride. Someone handed the little girl a pocket Bible to take home. The daughter said she'd give it to her grandma for she knew her grandma liked Bibles. The mother, however, grabbed the Bible away from the girl and threw it in the trash saying there wasn't enough room in the car for it. Later, the girl told her grandma about it.

What an opportunity, thought grandma. Avoiding any talk about the girl's mother's behavior, grandma spoke to her granddaughter about the precious treasure of God's word.

She described the words in the book as lit up and glowing throughout the world, throughout nature, glowing out of the hearts of many people the little girl could trust.

Grandma explained that even though this written book containing God's word was thrown into a trash can, that the living Word inside it can never be burned up or tossed away. In fact, God says His Word will never return void. His Word is living and will light up her soul if she bothers to read it asking God to make her understand it. Because the One who wrote the meaning in that book will listen to her prayer and help her know Him through that Word.

"Really?" asked the granddaughter.

Grandma made an installment of the great shivoo, or the mystery of this all-consuming truth, into her little one like planting a seed of the legacy she at one time also craved to know. She described that the Bible is not just a trinket to give to Grandma. It is not just an antique or a regular book, but that it has survived all the wars and all the schooling and all the ignorance of all humanity because it was written by the Creator of all humanity. He wants everyone to have an opportunity to know the stories represented by the small black marks on the page we call letters. These marks represent words and much deeper meaning on those pages.

Someone sorting through the trash would find this treasure now, and reading the strange meanings inside the cover, would find his or her brand new life waiting.

Grandma explained that the Word is alive like

dynamite, like a light in a scary tunnel, like a flashlight on a dark path people often find themselves walking, like the comfort of belonging the little girl felt in her grandma's arms. She held her grandbaby close then and prayed that God would speak these living things to the little one.

Inside the mind of the little girl, a light began to glow. The pilot light inside of the little girl was lit. A little curiosity grew into wild desperation to find that tossed away treasure. Craving it, she wanted to understand the mysterious power. She wanted to know her Creator. She salivated to read that Word, as she enjoyed the warmth of her grandma's embrace. The granddaughter would forget this story many days, but other days, she went searching with her whole heart for that most precious treasure.

She began talking to God about His path, and where she could find it in these days of curiosity and need. To think that she had once held the mystery in her hands, and her own mother had ripped it away and thrown it into the trashcan at a fairground! She might have lost it forever.

REASONING + WISDOM = CREATIVITY

I've noticed that traveling on vacation will break my habits and evacuate a stressful situation. Traveling sparks new and creative ideas for life. There was a time when King David's son, Absalom, created havoc in the kingdom, and David had to flee his home. Along the way, a man - crazy with rage - began to throw stones at David, cursing him for fleeing. David's mighty men were about to kill the enraged man, but David was traveling away from the havoc, I'm sure, pondering creative options. He said, "Wait. I don't know, and neither do you, whether the curses this man is shouting at me are from the LORD." David decided to wait for the counsel of time to see whether God would confirm.[3] What meekness he displayed! After all, David was king.

To develop this creativity in yourself is to develop leadership and problem-solving skills. We grapple with physiology, psychology, and the trajectory of our life.

Isn't it just too easy to halt a political conversation with an ultimatum or judgment? Yet, where does that lead? Often the relationship becomes walled up by judgment without attaining any path to higher ground. People often resist evil in vigilant inertia. But we are to project grace as we walk in truth.

This kind of living is not as easy as it would seem. Truth is the power of honesty setting us free, but to weave the truth into a compelling life story requires a clever hand. "You gotta know when to hold 'em, know when to fold 'em, know when to walk away, know when to run."[4] sang Kenny Rogers in The Gambler.

If someone gets in God's way, He figures it out. He lays a new path. He travels around and gets the job done. He creates glory anyway. Can we be like Him?

An aspect of grace is *charisma*, a divinely inspired gift conferring talent or power to lift something from the expected into the unexpected in transformation for good.[5] God endows charisma to whoever He chooses. Sometimes charisma comes through the humor of being human and admitting your need. Have you noticed? Traveling into transformation brings your initial list of observations to the next level of exploratory action, but *some awkwardness accompanies you into the unknown.*

The gift of the unknown is where we learn to walk in faith and trust the Guide's purpose. Only from our own perspective is the unknown a void. This space is actually where we are given special abilities.

As a helpful moth and a beautiful butterfly learn, life begins as a worm and takes a downward spiral into becoming larvae. Each creature then weaves a cocoon and goes into hiding. It eats away at the parts of itself it will never again need, losing so much of itself, it is transfigured into full charisma for a future life. When the time is right, each begins to stretch. Wings are strengthened for flight into the great unknown by pushing their way out of the cocoon. Apart from this struggle, the wings would never become strong enough to fly. Every part of the catharsis is needed to fly.

"God's sovereign call is for a purpose," Bob Deffinbaugh assures us. "It is not an aimless summons but a call to a certain destiny (see Isaiah 42:6, 43:7). That purpose is related to God's glory (Isaiah 49:1–3, 55:5). Since the gifts and the calling of God are intentional and irrevocable (Romans 11:29), we handle them with stewardship so that God's call on our lives is full of the glory of charisma

as we glorify our Sovereign. 'Surely My hand founded the earth, and My right hand spread out the heavens; When I call to them, they stand together' (Isaiah 48:13)."[6]

How has God been using a weakness combined with some other element in your life to transform your awkwardness into spiritual charisma?

Creatives suffer a particular difficulty finding their over-arching purpose. By the very nature of our life's work, we live in the swings and rollercoaster carts, emotional rollercoasters. In a single day, we may earn posters of praise while things fall apart left and right.

Do any artists you know live for the finality of a platform, a perfect performance, or being a single news item? Have you ever fallen for that golden temptation? How unprepared we are for the swift downfall of our carts every time we come off those rocket highs. As soon as a success is over, many of us turn to other ways to get that confidence and the high going again, and it seems any kind of high will do, even to our detriment and to the demise of those we love. Have you used substances to provide a high to escape the roller coaster of a creative life? What should a creative do to overcome the streams of depression, often despair and grab ahold of faith?

Since creatives don't see Jesus walking alongside us in person, it becomes of great importance to read the stories about Him in Scripture. When we insert ourselves into these stories and *hear* the testimonies of those who have struggled before us, we learn as they learned about God's abilities, His wonder-working power. For this, I was taught to pray "in Jesus' name."

Yet, a great connection of faith opened up to me when I began to understand the Biblical names of God beyond God the Father, God the Son, God the Holy Spirit.[7] There is no magic in saying, "in Jesus, we pray this..." but when we *invoke* the attributes of God, portrayed in the stories of Him as experienced by others, then we can petition the character of God. The One to Whom we pray comes into focus. Then, we are lifted out of our problem-focused views, our self-inflicted focus, into the powerful jurisdiction of this creative God. We can know *He sees* our predicament and can do something about it.

We can call on these names of God, these characteristics, with gratitude. Knowing the historical stories is of great benefit to our own posterity and to the legacy we will leave to others.

Have you written down a story about God's movements in your family or community or in your own life? These facts and wonders of God's supremacy prove that when we pray, even when we don't have the right words, His creativity is activated on our behalf. "Because the Spirit intercedes for the saints according to the will of God..." "all things work together for the good of those who love God and are called according to His purposes."[8] Tell that story first.

When the apostle Paul wrote the passage in Philippians 4, he set the ideal of *peace* to be the bookends of his passage.

Paul said to think on these things. First, he promised peace as a result of thankfulness to God. Then, being *kept* in peace is revisited at the end of his list.[9] Wouldn't it be nice to enjoy a steady sense of peace and perspective through the highs and lows of your creative career?

1. Whatever is true.
2. Whatever is honorable.
3. Whatever is just.
4. Whatever is pure. Keeping morally faithful saves us much suffering.
5. Whatever is lovely.
6. Whatever is commendable. What should be acknowledged? What is going forward on the right track, even though the effort has not yet arrived?
7. If there is any excellence, think on this: "Any excellence" shows the rarity of fine quality. If you know of a model of excellence, consider what makes the character or skill or performance or writing. Take notes.
8. Whatever is praiseworthy.[10]

Yes, these qualities exist in each of our lives. Paul is saying if you want peace, if you want the transforming power of God's peace to keep your heart and mind, then discover and meditate on the layers of goodness in your world. If they are attached to your network already, rejoice in the advantages. If these qualities are outside of your network, then grasp onto their tails.

Try this traveling exercise. Make yourself a shape by labeling all eight qualities above as the eight boundary lines of your shape. Whether you make a star or a free-form circle with the ideas, create some boundaries with these characteristics forming the circumference, taking the place of a line. These are your boundaries of *peace*. Even when you are not safe, even when your cart is flying down the slope of the rickety amusement park rollercoaster, you will have a traveling peace. Live inside the blessing of these eight walls of peace. Let them be your points of focus and shields of energy.

Let life's chips, distractions, critiques, and failures fall where they may. At each juncture, you may need to put a foot onto a new path. Take a baby step if that is all you can muster. Notice that the eight qualities travel with you. They are not fixed in time or place. So, venture out to create something new. Press on! Tweak or proof a second edition manuscript. Try out a new product in the industry. Take a new online course. Teach what you know.

The most important advice I can give you, though, is this: Whatever you do, do all things while giving thanks to God the Father. Nothing, I mean absolutely *nothing*, replaces your anxiety like thankfulness. Thankfulness opens the window to gratefulness, and gratefulness leads to new perspectives and to the joy of being rescued by our Savior.

As I was tooling around the lake this morning, I was thinking about how it would feel, what would it mean for David to have such an unthankful, untrue, scheming, slanderous, dishonorable son, Absalom.[11] The peace of God had left that house. After David's anointing, but before he actually became king, he had been pursued relentlessly by a crazy King Saul for years. Yet, as he traveled about he refused to retaliate. Instead, David confidently accepted that while God had anointed him, maybe his turn to rule hadn't yet come. He endured, *kept learning* and deferring to the sovereignty of God.

David was determined to be a good example as he roamed around the country chased by the Lord's anointed King Saul. David cleverly played protector and hero, and hid theatrically in the enemy's towns.[12]

How are you enduring your own unjust problem?

God's creativity is not stagnant. It moves with His own devices toward transformation. The peace of God is a *treasure*. In time, David went from herding sheep to warrior-king. Can you write about *His* timing? The very real struggle, and yet, all things became beautiful.[13]

EMBRACING IMPERFECTIONS IN OUR STORY

Improvisation. That's why we call it art, isn't it? We writers embrace imperfections in our written characters' thought patterns or behaviors so that the story can twist and turn just as much as it does in real life. Like jazz, development of a good story means the endings are strategically hidden in misunderstandings, physical barriers, or in something past. Discovering your own implicit historical bias will help you learn to use a story character's bias in his or her communications, meditation, or self-talk. Give them a starting place.

Can a writer empathize with the antagonist? A writer learns to love the enemy, maybe not the choices of the enemy, but a writer can sympathize with the person and the beginnings of the enemy. Did Jesus love Judas Iscariot?

You must learn about your antagonist's unique place of belonging or setting so that you can shape his or her believable thoughts, recognizable appearances or dialogue with accompanying accents and activities.

From an unlikely source or through an accident that turns out well, insight can emerge. Imperfections make your characters relatable. When you love them through their storytelling, you emulate God's love and faithfulness for our imperfect selves born into an imperfect world.

Even settings can wrestle for hope. Developing a setting can help hide or reveal your plot or your characters. The light we cast onto the flaws of our story characters is an act of kindness, though sometimes we create for them a severe mercy, as God sometimes does.

Did Hagar run to the desert to escape, only to be visited by the God of her hated mistress, Sarah? "I see you," God said. "Eat. Drink," and, "Go back to your hated mistress. I have a plan for you. Your own son will make a great nation because I have ordained it."

"Me?" Hagar said.

"Yes, Hagar, I see your need and your mistreatment. Yes, *you*," God said. So, Hagar dragged herself back to Abraham and Sarah. In faith. [14] And, God blessed her walk of faith.

When you draw on your own experience with fear or temptation, or from those close to you, you will understand that it is not impossible for the antagonist to be redeemed. Communicate that hope. If you determine to defeat the antagonist when thwarting the antagonist's purposes, you must *feel* that grief. It was written that Jesus loved the rich, young ruler who turned away.[15]

Proverbs 20:5 alludes that the purposes of a heart running like deep waters, but one with insight draws them out.[16] What is your character's point of view?

Imagine a master chef who creates a gourmet menu for a special entourage. She selects the best cuts of meat, the freshest organic grains to grind, the salad and herbs from her garden, and the cream from her cow. Someone sells her a tropical fruit, unknown to her, promising it will provide the hit. She shreds the fruit and tops the salad with it, only to discover that the fruit is poison.

"But everything I used was of the finest quality," she argues to the police.

"Everything except that shred of poison you added."

Use a shock point to hook the reader into how or why the poison was added, and by whom. Empathetically, draw the audience into the truth but do not dilute consequences. Make them meaningful.

When a writer can find the image of God originally shaped in the arch-type enemy, a starting point for where this character departed, the writer can make choices—or by other means have the character diverge from her image of origin and from her calling refusing to be rescued. When you know your bad character's history and psyche, you will draw her story accurately.

STEPPING THROUGH CRITICISM AND IGNORANCE

In teamwork, two things can destroy a person or a whole community: criticism and ignorance can ruin everything. The Donner-Reed Party learned this terrible truth as they tried to cut through an unknown mountain pass into California territory in early winter. Lacking cover and food, tragedy struck.[17] Ignorance and arrogance can beget a gruesome end.

Creating imaginative solutions requires an active faith, often teamwork, as iron sharpens iron, to defeat the fright of ignorance and arrogance. When ignorance and arrogance lead the way, those who follow often resort to powerless complaining and criticism. When life gets hard, frightened people are prone to criticize others, but finesse and talent may initiate a new course or a good reason to stay the course. "The purposes of a heart run like deep waters, but one with insight draws them out."[18] Even with properly appointed, qualified leaders, complaining can dismantle progress. As much as creativity pleases God, we read in Psalm 78 that complaining and slander will receive a just punishment. God dealt harshly with the Israelites for criticism and complaining. Group cooperation, then, is the key to producing a well-rounded result. Everyone must use their own voice to make this process meaningful. Can you name the ways a complaint is different than a proposal in a court setting or a mediation?

Unbelief is the underside of the coin "complaint." *Ingratitude* is the spine of that coin. After leading Israel out of bondage in Egypt by a series of wonders, miracles, and rescues, mind you, Moses continued toward the promised land. But people grew hungry and complained. So, God rained down manna. Then they complained that they would rather have meat, so He sent quail. Still, they slandered Moses, doubted God, and criticized, though they had caused their own enslavement.[19] When Mercy rescued them from Pharaoh's torments, they continued to grumble.

Prayer was an option. Rest was an option. A concert and dancing were options. A simple request in faith was an option, but apparently, nobody acted on any of these.

In order to show us how seriously God views griping, you can read both records in 1 Corinthians 10:9-11 and Hebrews 4:11, preserved for warnings to us. The Philippians also were taught to "do all things without murmuring and disputing."[20] In Matthew 15:19, Jesus associated slander with the violent sins that proceed out of a grossly wicked heart.

Many people experience the devastating effects of others who lie and complain about them to people in authority, to mutual friends, family members, or in city or county courts. Ephesians 4:31 asserts, "Let all bitterness, wrath, anger, clamor and evil speaking be put away from you with all malice." What Paul is talking about are the sins that destroy personal relationships. In

Proverbs 16:28 and Proverbs 17:9, Scripture says that slander utterly destroys friendships. Proverbs 18:8 and 26:22 says it leaves deep scarring wounds in the soul of the one slandered. Proverbs 26:20 reveals how criticism leads to conflict. And Proverbs 6:19, reveals the discord sown among a community. Can you write a paragraph or a song about this kind of relational violence?

Romans 14:3–5 indicates a creative alternative: "The one who eats [the ritual food of pagans] is not to regard with contempt the one who does not eat, and the one who does not eat is not to judge the one who eats, for God has accepted him. Who are you to judge the servant of another? To his own master he stands or falls; and he will stand, for the LORD is able to make him stand. One person regards one day above another, another regards every day alike. Each person must be fully convinced in his own mind." (NIV).

It's when a soft light shines over our darkness that we learn the power of forgiving ourselves. Gently. We are coaxed to peek into the corners of the closet when a kind voice asks or when the profound is tickled into laughter. It doesn't happen when we are berated in a storm of vitriol.

To overcome critical complaints, slander, and ungratefulness you'll need a cunning, winnowing faith. And the One who supplies all of our needs according to His riches in glory is the One who leads us safely to the prize.[21] Writers also understand that the characters they invent need an arc of development. The protagonist is not fully good, but complex, and the antagonist is not fully wicked, but a believable person with whom we can empathize in a motive or circumstance. Thus, the writer takes the reader, viewer, or listener on a personal journey of recognition (perhaps giving into temptation, or becoming heroic) with characters who are themselves being transformed.

The character who *is going somewhere* is the one who is alive, being transformed, and who finds a future and a hope. Be that person. The other may use magic and intrigue without the logos, but this technique leads only to a dead end.

Often the best writing just comes out of maturing experience. Writing about grace, talent, and power requires some knowledge, an understanding of the craft, and some divine wisdom for the application of it.

While an over-arching goodness abounds in a story accompanied by static darkness, the two are not parallel powers. God's goodness is always dynamic and creative. Both powers wrestle to win, and one may even appear to be moral or ethical, but only God's character maintains the living power leading to abundant life. Isaiah 9:8 says of God's kingdom and of His peace, there will be no end. His good will is ever expanding.

We don't like to experience difficult events in life. We don't enjoy perversion, betrayal or sickness. An assault or a series of losses can feel like the end of life as we hibernate through the waiting season—trying to feed our souls with skinny prey in chilly hunts, in odd, waking hours. We can't see beyond the one option that appears naturally before us.

That option may seem like a mountain. Gradually, oh, so gradually, we regain strength. We welcome spring's fresh bouquet, and we slowly roam the forest in the morning dew again. One night, an idea that has wiggled into the mind shouts at you. You simply have to find the time to explore it, to capture it, to story-board it. You feel the impetus. The gift must be transferred onto paper, and quickly, before the experience is lost.

When you are given such an idea, do you ask the Creator to transform any obstacles on your way up, as in helping you to use the rough places as cogs for a rail car climbing uphill? Ask Him to reveal the inner workings of this engine loaned to you. Do you research the source of energy for what He has given you to design? Do this for His glory. Investigate the angles.

Some designs take a velvet hand to implement. Others take a wrench to work and ply, others an explosion to be effective.

Some people bent in one direction may require a tranquilizer to calm them down, e.g., the raccoon whose fist is clenched around an object inside of a bottle-nosed trap desperately needs to let go in order to move on. Your experimental, artful voice might be the opening, the catalyst to a transforming power, in a member of the audience whom the Creator wants you to reach. Test the options. Question the obvious. Take baby steps.

Creation transforms continuously, even as we walk through the valley of the shadow of death.

Every morning, the LORD's faithful mercies are new[22], said the writer of Lamentations. He wrote this truth while living in captivity.

Because of God's daily activity to refresh us no matter where we find ourselves, we can also express

1) our trust in Him or

2) our misunderstanding of His reasons.

Admitting that both exist in our journeys toward transformation allows us to communicate the layers. When we are vulnerable in our own journey, other people open up. After King David sinned, he prayed, "Restore to me the joy of Your salvation."[23] He understood that he could not manufacture new hope or happiness by his own volition. His LORD was the source of all joy! Sorrow's tension is not the end of the story.

Wil Pounds says of Paul's thought in Romans 3:23, "The glorification of the Christian describes his complete and definitive conformity to the image of Jesus Christ."[24] We may practice this conformity as artists by copying His many expressions to us through nature's fruits and nature's seasons, or by depicting disasters and relief for disasters. We may express the Christ of creation in our skilled bodies, thoughtful minds, or through the unexpected kindness of an enemy or through observations of community. All belong to Him.

Suppose you had the innate ability to create a star. You spend years combining matter with chemicals. When the mass of the star is as big as a city, the only thing left for you to do is to launch the thing.

Launch it? Try as you might, you cannot figure out how to fling it into space and make it find a place of belonging in the universe.

Finally, you say to God, "Look! I did what you asked, but it seems silly now. I can't launch it. What is the purpose? Do what you will with all these efforts, and all my vain striving."

When you turn it over to the Creator, you go home to get some rest.

That night the LORD blows in a miraculous wind. The force begins to roll the star-in-the-size-of-a-city up the mountain canyon. The star begins to spin as it picks up velocity and speed. Heating, it begins to glow, and suddenly it simply lifts into the air and flies away into the place appointed for it. You watch all this from your bedroom window. In your excited state, you realize God not only gave you the ability and provided the materials, but He was the only one Who could give it place and purpose.

In effect, you could do nothing apart from Him. He breathed life into the symbol of a star. He gave it real function. This is exactly the mystery of God's Spirit functioning in our lives. The Spirit fuels and transforms the things we do as we explore the aims of God's Word. Sometimes people refer to this special effect as "an anointing." We can mimic His creativity and let it flow out of us like a funnel, a channel of truth, offering a sentiment that can only be made through our own spiritual journey—which is to Him, and to many others, a work of art.

God calls all of His creation His servants, because He has a purpose for our existence. He is the Re-namer, and Redeemer, and Re-purposer. When we walk with the LORD, consider the possibilities limitless. We can search for Him—though He is not far from any of us. Coming closer to our Creator, we can accept His call to be cunning and skillful. We can even become His friend.

Anything can become the next exploration. Even those creatives who want nothing to do with being a child of God often find their best material in Scripture and in the church. God can use the imagination of anyone to teach us.

Your own skill is a learned thing. Wisdom takes time. You may not yet understand this when you begin to write about a tragedy causing a family to become displaced, all their treasures to be lost. What you are really going to discover and write about is the greater gift of creativity from loss, the value of new relationships, and community—finding other treasures in hidden places. This story may require much prayer, wrestling with God for the blessing, and many edits to test and strengthen the wings. This is how our author, Lynn Byk, wrote *Mister B: Living With a 98-Year-Old Rocket Scientist.*[25]

When we learn our lessons, we realize that we are prepared to lead, administrate, and be creative in journaling!

THE TRANSFORMING BEAUTY OF TEAMWORK

King Solomon understood the difficulties and the joy of becoming King of Israel. He praised the Lord for the benefits, but he also prayed for knowledge and wisdom.

"For who can rule this people of Yours?" he prayed. God granted Solomon great wisdom and knowledge. For the rest of us, He grants teamwork.

Sometimes I wish there existed a prism of myself. There is just too much for one person to do! Who else would know how to pick up and complete any aspect of what's on my plate to accomplish today? This is especially true when it comes to the mysterious aspects of marketing or getting the word out. But, God provides teamwork! In His provision of teamwork, God has cleverly drawn us to *fellowship*–which we are instructed to have in His Word.

When I was a young person, I wrote a song, using my guitar, about the prophet Jeremiah. I saw it rolling out like a heavy metal rock opera. "Jeremiah! How long did ya cry? How did ya suffer, and how did ya die?" It traveled through a melancholy verse in a minor key and set the stage for a tale of fairly dramatic woe.

Instead, this song rolled out the sliver of breath delivered by a soprano choir girl's voice. What could have happened if a parent, youth leader, coach, or teacher had heard the song and rallied a band of instruments together to ignite the potential of that lyric, that idea? The seed could have been watered with teen artists painting backdrops, musicians trading out talent for posters and a platform, and a possible tour of the Northwest. But pulling together such a team required the vision and a hefty dedication of someone in a position to rescue, and someone with significant wisdom to help a child thrive.

Nurturing creatives often means creating teamwork; hiring editors, designers, and stagehands; building an audience, and building tenacity, in layer upon layer. This is *transformation*. Learning to share and to hear the wisdom of others are two of the most valuable skills a transformational artist acquires. Making others a priority is transformative to your own character and your own story.

Perhaps you invent the prototype of something great, but it needs to be chiseled into existence or brought to life by someone else who can take it to the next level. Often, taking something to the next level requires a nurturing mentor, a teacher with insight and opportunities at hand, or a parent to discover and push the creative person along—prodding and pulling the cart for supplies and audiences and awards until the artist gains a deserving platform for a creator. Two are stronger than one. Although it is difficult to turn over a new piece to the next in line for the next creative touch in the process, use, or promotion; a wise creative eventually sees the beauty of teamwork.

While practicing creativity in your family or community, do you honor the inspiration and Biblical creativity of others? Do you tell others when something is said or done by them to turn on a light in your mind?

Working on your creative output with a partner is just as spiritual a discipline as giving to the poor or taking care of one's parents in their old age.

Creativity is self-exploration in community in its rarest, raw forms. You are unique. But you may die on the vine if you do not plug into the matrix and become vulnerable to others and also a servant to their needs. And, I assure you, this takes courage and deliberation.

What journey has God given to you to express to others? Are you taking steps to arrive at your goal?

People who create are exploring God's creation, and the person of God as He reveals Himself. Makers and creators do this as we become God-mimickers. Those who create are the children of God acting like their Father. And those who have no time to be creative—to read, to paint, to sing, to act, to memorize or to write— have no time to develop spiritually.

As a managing partner of a developing boutique publishing group, I had to learn the language of a publisher: how to obtain a Publisher's Cataloging-in-Publication, a Library of Congress Control Number, an International Standard Book Number, Book Industry Subject and Category codes for subject headings, publisher's lingo for formatting, and strategies for prepublication Advanced Readers Copies. I had to find and hire editors and learn how to recognize a good story despite the flaws. I had to learn how to cull a 50-word description from a verbose description for an advertising blurb. I had to learn how to invite new authors to invest in profile pictures and motivate them to begin using social media sites. I learned the hard way and the expensive way to record an audiobook, then two of our authors were picked up and gifted audiobooks! I had to learn how to pick metadata, fonts, and illustrators. I had to deal with bias from traditional publishers and bookstores who needed to be sold. I learned to budget and to account for royalties, how to be a good steward of the small things. I learned these things from other communities and applied them for the good of my team.

Not generally being a person of finesse, *these were things I didn't particularly want to learn.* In fact, because I lacked a passion for business and because I am not naturally gifted in detail work and because it seemed to me that the labor was far more demanding than the reward, I had a crisis of faith, wondering whether God had called me to work at Capture Books.

I forewarned the authors that I was seeking the LORD for a month. And that's only the beginning of how I kept on seeking Him.

Out of those four weeks, though, came the notes to this book, a trip to the New York Book Expo, and a lot more quiet time. I met two new authors. Out of it also came a financial model of sustainability from one author, Sue Summers. The confirmation was overwhelming. My world has expanded from a poet's hermitage and writers' group facilitator, to a business partner with a growing network of team players who try to help each other from the heart. "You did not choose me, but I chose you and appointed you so that you might go and bear fruit— fruit that will last- and so that whatever you ask in my name the Father will give you. This is my command: Love each other."[26]

Do you ask, *what if?* Does your personal work expression reflect movement from point A to point B? How do you offer a step in your journey to transform a situation for your audience?

Kathy Joy's series, *Breath of Joy*, is an example of transformation. In her collection of season-themed, inspirational books, she walks us through her spiral of despair from being a successful Colorado D.J. to enduring an obedient move with her husband. He moved his family into his dream on his family's farm in Pennsylvania. In his sudden cardiac arrest, Kathy Joy felt her abandonment and displacement was complete. Raising two teen daughters in yet another home far away from joy as she understood it, she shows her readers how she survived. She does this through not more than a dedication of her book, the rest being speaking wonder in her content, moments of everyday celebrations which were creative exercises for her own survival.

These wonders transport the reader into joy because of her intentionality to find beauty in survival.

Many people want to become the next star, diva, or idol, but the point of art is to experience the therapy, to experience the change that takes place inside. Art between two people depicts a true, sacred testimony.

Christian art is more than humanistic in its aim.

The hero or heroine is that way, not because they are inherently lovely people, but because something wonderful about God becomes known. Christian storytelling includes the dimension of God's breath entering into a life like a wind tumbles the tumbleweed. It always differentiates the meekness of the little c — creator and the blessedness of the big C — Creator.

Today, I found myself printing the term, *RESPONSIBILITY*, in a gratefulness journal given to me by author, Tracy Fagan. Responsibility has brought me friendship, taught me teamwork and strategy, and how to be meek, and loads of other savvy bits of wisdom. When I push through difficulties for the love of others, for the tenor of God's voice, my personal rewards grow.

Every book, whether a picture book or a story book or a hymn book, embarks on a journey. That journey often mirrors your personal journey with others.

IMAGES FOR COMMUNITY AND PERSUASION

Some say that God's image was the image of a unified front, a passionate community, one God, three persons recording together (John 5:7, Galatians 4:1–7). Community causes communication. Thus, an ability to relationally communicate for a unified, higher purpose is what the image of God means for us. We are created in and for community. This is His image.

When artists create in tandem with other artists, or in teamwork with other specialists, many challenges occur. It is both harder and the returns are better. Potential for greater communication to a wider audience also occurs. Teamwork is challenging, but it can reap rich rewards for bonding in a mutual aim and self-exploration, as well as understanding others' needs, gifts, and purposes. It gives Christian artists the opportunity to serve others with their performances and lift up the talents of the team's efforts in a broader matrix of expression.

Communication among Father, Son, and Holy Spirit is the model for our own expression. They think the World of each other. They decide things together—like how to fling the stars into place and how large the orbits of planets should be—and they laugh at each other's ideas, while spreading glory over their implementation of God's expression in the Earth (Gen. 1:2, John 1:1–3). Can artists and non-artists find this kind of unity, too? Unity is a primary goal for His creation.

The best art is art that communicates intricacy, ambiance, or inspiration to another. The best art turns on a light in the soul of another.

GROUP GROWTH THROUGH SINGING

Can you explain why a certain song playing under a passage in a radio drama or audio book evokes a deep response in you? Why does a song bring a specific pathos or comedy to a movie script? Musicians and sound engineers work diligently to provide a specific psychological interpretation, but they craft in mysteries that cannot be unpacked with mere words. It's an exploration of intervals, tones, rhythms, orchestration, and keys. They translate tangibles into intangible ideas and create emotions which, in turn, have the power to seed changes in human thought and human values.

Hearing the power of music which supported words, a curriculum for singing the Psalms throughout the year was developed at Capture Books. The Psalms books also help people memorize the testimonies and thoughts of spiritual ancestors. There is the regular *Psalm Hymns: Dramatic, Contemplative, Singable, Recitable Psalms!,*[27] and there is a holiday adaptation called *Caroling Through the Psalms.*[28] Both are transformative tools, full of opportunity for fun and teamwork as well as discussion opportunities to learn about God through theology and history. Singing the Psalms introduces questions that create character and faith in a person.

Advent, a ritual of transformation from silence and ignorance, can give students an opportunity to know, *to personally sit in the place of,* the Hebrews before Christ's arrival in the flesh. Doubt is dispelled in a knowledge that works backward to this God, Emmanuel, Who is now with us in flesh. Using *Caroling Through the Psalms* will take Advent into a whole new pattern of experience.

Assign choral members a psalm-carol to ripen for performance to develop many curious minds and team experience. Assign students a dramatic recitation to memorize to provide a memorial backdrop in their own journey. Maybe you'll be credited for starting the first singing Bible study. For creatives, the discovery of our ancestors' personal experiences offer us some unique pieces of sacred work to help establish a professional portfolio as a stage actor or singer.

The Psalms were meant to be sung. In context, the Psalms inform us of the extraordinary expressions of a variety of relationships with God prior to His coming in the flesh. And many of them are so dramatic that they lend themselves to dance or theater or evening liturgies.

LIVING INTENTIONAL LOGOS FOR GROUP GROWTH

All our attitudes and words are important. Each one leads to redemption in Christ or to desolation. We are told that we will give an account for every idle word (our logos) one day. Here is the context of that verse:

> "The good man brings good things out of his good store of treasure, and the evil man brings evil things out of his evil store of treasure. But I tell you that men will give an account on the day of judgment for every careless word they have spoken. For by your words you will be acquitted, and by your words you will be condemned."[29]

Here, the "idle word" is translated as "careless;" it can literally mean "lazy word." However, if we circle around the phrase to study it, the meaning becomes not so much that a word is dribbling from the mouth of an inert person, but that the expression is not a responsible one, or clever. It is stuck in the mud of inertia. It offers nothing of the Logos, no expounding revelation. There's no life in it. Without life, even true words will condemn.

If you happen to be a resourceful and prosperous artist yourself, are you mentoring, sponsoring others? All of our expressions need some life-giving energy to travel well and far. So, avail yourself of this incredible life-giving power of the Logos to transform. The meek open hands of a mentor will welcome a learner.

Have you considered the intent of Romans 8:18–21? Here, the Apostle Paul says that all creation is waiting in expectation for the Children of God, for the glory to be revealed in us. In fact, the One who subjected it to frustration did so *in the hope that creation itself will be liberated from its demise with the transformation of souls.* Wow! How's that to happen in the context of our ongoing, developing sanctification here on Earth?

Your glorification for each good work in Christ Jesus, while spoken of in the past,[30] lies in the future, between the lines, so open your hands. Wait. Wait on the LORD while going about the functions of your common day listening, experimenting, and discovering.

Like getting a blood transfusion, new living DNA is injected into the veins of new believers. With it, we are charged with a responsibility to correct the trajectory of creation's decay--to lead nature out of enslavement--on the road of corruption into a new liberating way to glory. As the children of God, all of this is under our charge even as we are also actively transforming into our own glory. As God enlightens us, we are to practice resuscitating acts and rescuing powers in this Earth.

How do the children of God make this difference? We ask for, and humbly practice, the wisdom of God given in stagnant situations. For example, a group may try to protect environments from adverse impact, but many other aspects of creation may become adversely affected. Recall the introduction of wolves and lynx into the Northwest, or protecting the rodents in California, or erecting windmills and flying airplane turbines into the flight paths of birdlife, or the effect of certain chemical applications to grains at harvest? The House of God is charged with finding creative, better alternatives to preserve and liberate all of creation.

Consider the phrase, "only what's done for Christ will last." Is this maxim limited to terms of evangelism? What of the trees, rivers, and rocks clapping their hands in praise to the Creator Christ? Colossians 1:16–17 and John 1 display the Creator-Redeemer as worthy of being praised. (See also, Isaiah 44:23–24.) Anything we do in conjunction with the purposes of our Creator is a worthy, whole gift to glorify the LORD in society.

Whether you find yourself creating art in the sanctuary, like the priest Ezra,[31] or you find yourself creating art in the city, like Nehemiah (men who were contemporaries of each other),[32] God considers both as good works when done at His bidding for those He loves, and at His disposal. Like in any job, a particular form of creativity is meant for a specific use. Some good works are meant for general worship, others are meant for personal ministry or specific education of age groups, and still others are meant for general business or civic uses. "For I am confident of this very thing, that He who began a good work in you will perfect it until the day of Christ Jesus."[33]

Rule 3: HOPE. Ask, *what if?* Train your eye to transformation. Aim in every step to make tributaries to the purpose, praise, and priorities of God.

4

TO COMMUNICATE

As the singer, Glen Campbell, entered into aphasia at the end of his battle with Alzheimer's disease, his daughters and wife reported that he could no longer use his words or understand others' words. But Glen could still receive happiness and love from their touch, from controlled temperatures, and from the work of keeping him free of bedsores. He sang things to himself in his own world. It seemed music and being fed dessert remained a means of deep personal satisfaction to him.[1] When I read this account, I was reminded how deeply people understand things and can respond without the advantage of words.

When I am enjoying a restaurant, it is often due to the musical atmosphere and the table settings, adequate spacing and cleanliness. Subconsciously, all these elements work together to either put me at ease and create joy or they work to repel me. All *this*, before I pick up the menu!

I recently learned that key Bible stories are being translated into 400 sign languages for the deaf around the world. The program that is helping to make this happen is cued to "see" and "translate" from 65 points of expression on a face. See, sign language depends as much upon facial expression as it does upon hand signals.

Language is complex. Expressing yourself among a variety of cultures, each having inflections, and different communication styles, is like the user of an Apple operating system trying to communicate with an old IBM user or a biased Windows PC user. When your name isn't "God"—you can bet, it isn't—communication takes work! Look at the root of the idea, though. It starts with community. Technically, we should be able to *hear* one another because we hold some basic values in common.

> **In the beginning**, do you think the **void** was *silence* or *space*?
>
> Was the **void** a reference to a *lack of chemical combustion* or *suspended electrical currents*?
>
> Was the **void** an *absence of minerals or water specifically related to the beginning of Earth*?
>
> Was the **void** a *want* in God's nature to communicate to another?
>
> We know there was *darkness* hovering. Did the *light* come to fill up the deep darkness? Was it only because of *light* that humans could see?

Communication is a conversation. Innovation often begins by opening the avenues of communication before we learn the song and lingo needed to articulate our interests and concerns to one another. Artistry can make or break the flow of our ability to hear each other.

When the goal is to open up a sympathetic avenue of understanding, we're told to ask open-ended questions to help move a dialogue along. Asking questions of mutual concern opens up gates of respect. These intersections of mutual values can open up new understanding, which can also turn on the flow of creative juices.

I used to volunteer as a music therapist at Craig Hospital. "Locked in" is what we called brain injured patients who were unable to communicate with others. When the brain injured were unable to respond, my musical partner and I would play their favorite music. Hearing the music would enable the patient to make physical responses with their thumbs or fingers or by blinking their eyes or looking to the right or left. It let us know that cognition was alive and that there was hope for more sophisticated communication. The white matter in the brain began to connect injured hemispheres.

True artistic inspiration consists of two-sided communication. The breather's expression flows from one person into sensitive ears, recognition to the eyes, tastes on a tongue, or as a scent to a nose. Information flows from the one who is touching to another being touched and into the mind of the recipient. Yet, sometimes layers of meaning in a story or parable are not unraveled until the audience is in a position to plumb its depths.

Noise pollution and media gimmicks rumble around as an undercurrent to life and often blaze at us, distracting us from what matters. Can the brain quickly absorb speeding data? Sure. Is it healthy?

Our minds can become sluggish in distinguishing how to capture the wind in our sails, which tact we should take, and to what aim.

Communication of priority can be subtle, quiet, uncanny. God doesn't shout like a *Klausomaniac* unless He wants to. Neither do we. God uses twilight and midnight to speak with a different tone of voice than when He does at daybreak or in the pressure of desert heat or, in a whipping, decentralizing whirlwind.

What He is saying may require that we listeners participate in earnest by seeking His voice and entering into the quiet.

Did you know that entering into a regular space of rest is the sacred commandment most often broken? This is because rest requires discipline to quiet down. Life's urgencies need to be physically quieted in order to gain the greater experience. Try to enjoy some artistic reflection in the LORD on a regular basis, rest on Sabbath. Enjoy it with a friend or family member. Rest, reflect, and trust God to make it good.

There are also other sacred ordinances. When we think of them, we see communion, marriage, and baptism. Really, all three ordinances are theater pieces depicting God's relationship with His beloved. No matter where you fall theologically, you cannot escape that these rites—or dramas—these celebrations, are more theatrical than verbal communication and are better symbols of relationship than letters on a page. Part of the work belonging to a Christian creative, then, is depicting or reenacting these mysteries to new audiences by new means.

To be called "Christian drama" in genre is to depict the intent of a Creator-God becoming deeply and personally involved in life.

TWO MEANS OF RECEIVING

Empirical data is what teachers often use to impart knowledge. Using words to define history, or instruct on a process, or to present facts to students, tends to aptly incorporate maxims of philosophy or theology, mathematics, and science. These can then lead to ultimatums, channels, formulas, standards, and more statistics. Heady stuff. Empirical data includes exact definitions of terms in linguistics. This does not mean that connotations of words and ideas are irrelevant or to use them, heretical.

However, another way to learn is through *experience*. For example, we may toss around the word *honor*, but until we experience a personal honor ourselves, we don't truly understand how the reward lifts and separates it from the not-so-honorable. Nor do we ever face our natural responses to an honor, whether it be humility or pride, in order to note intersections of humanity unless we, at some interval, experience honor ourselves. Experience allows us to follow the dots into the unknown. We learn from intersecting paths along the way. We learn to improvise.

For years, I was conflicted about the way religious people interchanged the terms "forgiveness" and "reconciliation". This was because there were situations in my own life, and in the lives of those I loved, which prevented reconciliation—even though we practiced forgiveness. Finally, a wise teacher explained that there are times when the experience of reconciliation is not possible, either because the offender has not changed behaviors and attitudes—and is dangerous, or because the offender is no longer alive or within reach, or because the offender refuses to be reconciled. When I took inventory, I understood the differences immediately and years of confusion and imposed guilt were lifted from me.

Similarly, someone may teach us the definition of repentance, but until we go through the experience of being seen in our financial, emotional, or spiritual nakedness, and experience the necessary heartfelt process of repenting, we do not understand the transforming power of its meaning. Furtively, we define the term "graciousness," but we won't understand the physiological warmth that flows through a gracious person unless we become the recipient of their incomprehensible act.

Now somewhere between these two means of learning (empirical data and personal experience), is the concept of storytelling. Storytelling takes the empirical data to a new level of meaning. It does this by focusing on an application of the idea being communicated. By moving the data or idea inside a variety of situations, storytelling acts much like using a connotation to expand definitions into a culture or into human understanding. Connotations bring much understanding to a term because of the broader idea.

Using industry lingo also applies important detail when writing or portraying action or dialogue in any particular industry. Foregoing the lingo will make too much of a concession to your authority of the subject matter, but using it may confuse or alienate an audience unfamiliar with the culture. It falls to the creative to include particular descriptions, stories, pictures, or actions to lead the audience into understanding. If you need detail about police life, interview a law officer. If you need detail about what it feels like to be paralyzed in given situations, ask a quadriplegic. If you want to know why a person would become a prostitute, engage one in a conversation, and ask.

Full expression of the description, action, history and attitude are explored because this is where the poetry of life is found.

Spontaneous combustion happens when we receive an emotion from an image or a series of images, or characters, and we partner with the raw elements with symbols or notes on a page, with history or science to express the revelation. Only then can we express the news or an angle on the news. We can retell the story of what moved us in a variety of ways, whether by memoir, or through a fictional tale, or by a few strokes of the pencil, by dance movement, or by spinning a tune with newly punctuated color and rhythm.

Then, invited into a new application of art, others may open up receptive windows of the brain to hear a new sound or see a new sight, and mentally connect new thought-dots.

The skill with which we are able to express ourselves, is the creativity that woos another mind and another's will to open up even a back door, to at least privately consider something we deem important.

Not only did God tell stories, but Jesus told parables. At least one person, though, has challenged me, "If you are a Christian publisher, then why do you sell *fiction*?" If this question were asked you, how would you answer?

I was reading ADORNING THE DARK by Andrew Peterson about his own creative path, and he described how he was drawn to Watership Down, Middle Earth, and The Pendragon Chronicles, actually any book he could find with a fantasy cover. His grandmother didn't understand what drew him away from his studies and his chores or simple conversations with others.

He discerned that she thought it might be the sex in those books. But that wasn't it at all. Most had no sexual content. He described that during the hours he spent reading these books, he was transported into another world with other characters holding swords and defined situations of good and evil where, with careful planning, good friends, and trusty daggers, good would always conquer the evil and things would be set right as clearly as if he had fallen through the wardrobe into Narnia.

Coming back to reality was simply tragic. There

were no dragons to fight. He was not yet out of middle school, high school, or college.

Peterson's description of his time of youthful discontent, bored with the real world, had the effect of sticking pins into my soul. This same discontent and boredom was exactly the void into which I also dropped fantasy books during formative years. For some reason, growing up and encountering real-life dragons takes so many hundreds of days in middle-class America, that these books, along with Star Wars and Star Trek and other time travel movies, offered the art and experiences we knew must be out there. This immersion into fantasy was the navigational wisdom we longed for.

We want to identify with the good characters, but sometimes, we understand the bad characters all too well. And this is the power of fiction writing. It doesn't hide reality and truth from us. It brings truth into a time and space where the deeper stories of life can be taken out and handled, turned round and set under a microscope for our examination.

This week, I've been walking my dog and weeping a little, trying not to have a pity-party for all that hasn't happened to me in my lifetime. Some people cry about all the things that *have* happened to them. What I do know is, things move so slowly. And, we have limited vision.

We experiment with art and use it for personal therapy, and we don't know that later, down the road, we'll be mortified to pull out what we've produced in the past and listen to what others must have heard, cringing for having published it. We move through life and love, also putting up boundaries against encroaching evil in simple, finite manners.

We don't know how far-reaching our personal dragon-slaying events will be. Only God has that kind of omniscience. And sometimes an author, poet, or filmmaker will adorn the dark.

On a continuum, do you learn better through experience or through empirical data? On another continuum, do you express yourself better through modeling or through teaching data?

There are times a storyteller needs to develop a story because the storyteller needs to process it as the communicator *and* the receiver. We call this process, "art therapy." Sometimes, though, it can be even more profound. Have you ever received a treasure from the LORD for your own benefit while trying to be creative making something for others?

> What are some biblical examples of "storytelling" for a higher purpose?

Even if no one else gets to hear, read, or see it, putting pencil to paper is valuable because of the spiritual journey it takes you through. Philippians 2:12–13 says, "continue to work out your salvation with fear and trembling. For it is God who works in you to will and to act on behalf of His good pleasure." Whether you earn a living in art or become a known household name is not nearly as important as just processing the gift.

NAMING AND PLACING

Sometimes an artist doesn't understand what he or she is communicating until a piece gets surrounded by context or gets named. The irony is applied like the highlights to a painting in the final moments when the piece is unveiled. What if the work has mocked the city in which the gallery is located? Placement and the name each form the heightened message. Every preceding preparation culminates at the naming and placement.

Naming and context provide succinct meaning, creating a specific power, putting the cherry on top of a sundae.

We understand the one who gives the name is greater than the person or thing being named. God names and inventories all of His starry hosts.[2] In the first chapter of Genesis, God named day and night.[3] In the next chapter, Adam, who was created in resemblance to God, named each animal[4] and also named the other part of him, "Eve."[5] And God revealed names to us, and a gender, by which He prefers to be known. This is His sovereign prerogative.

The Word of God called some things evil, some wicked, some righteous, some common, some holy. Religious converts may hear these terms and labels without any context, differentiation, or understanding of what they mean and why the labels apply. In centers of some religious thought, to throw out the terms and definitions seems like the more politically correct and inclusive option.

I wonder if God continues to have the prerogative to name things in His world.

When a person is labeled a Christian, the label becomes a matrix of meaning to all those who live in the context of that person's attitudes and actions. Say a troubled kid enters the picture. His whole demeanor shouts, "troubled" and "perverse". You have the choice of communicating either,

a) "We don't associate with people like you," or

b) "I also have a story about need. At my disposal are all the resources of the Creator and His kingdom, and I intend to invite you into my story and practice showing you this creative, corrective grace that the Savior gave to me and reaches from me because of love."

The second attitude communicates a path leading from mutuality into mercy and hope. You figure out healthy boundaries, or find aid, and teach forgiveness. "Likewise, every good tree bears good fruit, but a bad tree bears bad fruit."[6] When your response reflects a desire to help another lost soul to find a future, your Christian label begins to glow with a prism of new color.

Bob Deffinbaugh reminds us of the bookend of transformational communication in that, "God not only names, He also renames. God changed the names of Abram and Sarai to Abraham and Sarah (Gen. 17:5, 15). The LORD Jesus changed Simon's name to Cephas or Peter (John 1:21). The new name given is indicative of a new destiny, brought about by God" who controls human destinies (*See* Isaiah 4, 56:5, 62:2, and 65:13–15, Jeremiah 19:6, Daniel 1:7; and Revelation 2:17).[7]

Should a flow of consciousness overtake your original plot due to a new character's fleeting joy, should your characters demand the unexpected because they've noticed a facial expression you didn't see in your first draft, should God breathe His own layers of purpose into your work, then allow yourself to follow the breadcrumb trail to learn something new of subtle communications?

VALUE YOUR CREATIVE IMPRESSIONS

What is Creativity? To me, it is the combination of imagination and work. How would you define it?

Do you respect artists whose work does not claim Christ in any form of the inspiration? Has God communicated to you through them? God's Word, whether tacit or direct, does not return to Him empty. It will accomplish what the Creator set out for it to do regardless of the messenger He uses to convey what He wants to say.[8] Thank God for the mastery of skill He gave to the one who goes before you. Bring to your mentors and teachers the respect and honor due, even payment due, for the ways in which they have inspired you on your journey.

If you want your own communication to be rich and lasting, trust that God is infusing His expression into your own life. You may want to inventory the points and landmarks of truth and inspiration as a list of eye-openers. Keep a journal nearby. Trust Him, as you work, to mingle every good thing and carry it to where it best makes sense. He has an audience in mind.

When Anne Rice authored *Called Out of Darkness: A Spiritual Confession,*[9] it was a departure from all of her vampire storytelling. God used this mysterious work of Anne's conversion to spark in me the conviction that music is a complete holy, artful expression without lyrics. It awakened in me the knowledge that God authorized and speaks through art in mysteries.

Anne was able to unleash, in her autobiography, images of God's hand invoking life from yearning. In the lines of her descriptions, roses tumble from stone walls and childhood paths to Him are lined with fallen petals. Her yearnings sought for an intersection with God's symbols. From her muted childhood dilemmas through her atheistic adulthood and earthshattering losses, Anne transported me along her journey. We walked toward a holy mystery of artful repurposing. Image and word, music without words, invoking the Redeemer's mercies upon the dead.[10]

G. K. Chesterton's story, *The Ball and the Cross*, begins with a science-fictional opening as critical of evolution as anything written today. It provides a story of salvation without using a "sinner's prayer" and, toward the end, it unveils a miraculous divine intervention.[11]

Our Creator transformed pertinent aspects of His expression into illustrated forms of Himself when he spoke into the silence. When He formed Adam, then Eve, in His own Image, they were not created by using King James symbols of language. They were breathed into being.[12] The first Adam experienced the garden and his relationship to God and to his wife prior to knowing any language. Then, God taught the couple a language with which He could call out to them.

The problem is, of course, image being image and the word being word, that hard work is required for the translation between left brain and right brain camps to occur. We must learn to use, and to honor, communication through images, senses, and the use of humor as well as communicating through words.

Did God purposely set up a communication dilemma? It is tempting to be harsh and critical of others who disagree with you, and it is difficult to accept harsh criticism from others who do not "get where you are coming from" or where you are going. But, maybe telling

WHY do you think God would set up various forms of sacred expression – nature, non-verbal human expression, versus language?

a story can serve to highlight a point and let the chips fall where they may. I've told many stories that I didn't even know were inside me, but telling them to others made me realize how the LORD was moving in new ways. None of us will agree fully with another human being, but story-telling bridges many gulfs with new understandings on both

sides. Your experience and own impressions matter. But don't take them so seriously that you cannot be touched by a story.

Anyone interested in complementarian versus egalitarian roles, male/female gender issues in the Church, business, and home, understands that constant friction arises from the question of how God's image in humans appears, whether it was placed only in the male, or in both the male and female and what—pray tell—does that declaration of the image of Logos really imply?

Image, direct or indirect, has always presented some sore points of discussion. Doesn't He know He formed dissension rather than a clear link to communication? It's puzzling. "All Scripture (including implied parts or parts demurring) is God-breathed and is useful for teaching, rebuking, correcting and training in righteousness," wrote Timothy's mentor, Paul, in 2 Timothy 3:16. On the other hand, our glorification is certain,[13] yet *unseen.*[14] And, faith is the *substance* of things unseen.[15] Did God leave His fingerprint, or does He continue to leave fingerprints every day through ongoing creativity?

As the recipient, do not accept the tone of harsh criticism from anyone in your artistic exercises, even though you must accept the discipline of genuine critique and criticism. Harsh treatment can kill the many stages and fun in a creative journey. Quenching a human spirit is an act of war against the creative impulse God Himself authorized and thoroughly enjoys in us.

Creatives may give up what is most childlike and precious to them and to God when life is censored and spiritualized, void of play, with harshness as the reward.

Harshness is reserved for warnings of a fire or a knife aimed at someone's back or a rope unraveling from which you are tethered. It is a tone used to incite the fight-or-flight response.

If someone is harsh with their tone for any other reason, it is more about them than it is about you. Maybe they have lost their value for childlikeness or maybe they are inexperienced in mentoring. Maybe they haven't eaten food recently. Offer food. Keep playing.

GOOD IMAGE IN FLESH

The original concept of the word "image" in Hebrew meant "shade." God created a shade or shadow of Himself in our species. When God created humanity in His image, His Son was not yet born in the flesh, so unless you set time aside, it is difficult to say that God created us in His physical, genetic image or gender. God is Spirit. "In His image" if not a reference to physical bodies like that of Jesus Christ, must refer to will, emotions, goodness, mental acuity, communication, and relationship. Perhaps it refers to a sense of glory. Perhaps it refers to the ability to create.

In Genesis, He pronounces all of His created images in nature, in the universe, and in Adam and Eve, "GOOD." He smiled, pumped the air with special energy, and sat back to watch us settle in for a day of pleased restfulness. Then, when He sent His Son, the Word was again made flesh, the second Adam was sent, God in flesh, for a highly specific form of goodwill and necessity.

God sanctioned flesh good for the second time. Again, God thundered from heaven, "This is my beloved Son in whom I am well-pleased."[16]

This pleasure included all the eating and defecating functions of a body as well as the pierce-able flesh, breakable bones, spill-able blood, and physical chemistry of Christ's flesh. Ask around. Is one bodily function more sacred than the other?

Artists and medics, parents and lovers inherently acknowledge that the human image is sacred, even when it is diseased, broken down, or when, for specific purposes, it is maligned. We are full of secret wonders.

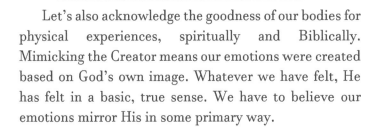

Exactly which emotional experiences are *ungodly*, do you think?
a) Write a list detailing when it might be appropriate to feel each emotion you can imagine.
b) How would God relate to these feelings Himself?
c) Try to write a list of the holy facial expressions of God if He had a face, and another list of unacceptable emotions.

Let's also acknowledge the goodness of our bodies for physical experiences, spiritually and Biblically. Mimicking the Creator means our emotions were created based on God's own image. Whatever we have felt, He has felt in a basic, true sense. We have to believe our emotions mirror His in some primary way.

Do you ever feel *guilty* for being sad? Bored? Overwhelmed? Enraged? Sexual? Passionate? Sloppy? Happy? Have you wondered whether Christians are supposed to feel these *unleashed* emotions? Can these experiences be said to be fundamentally beautiful expressions of life in God?

Do you feel guilty when you are furiously tempted to destroy an enemy, or abuse someone of the opposite gender? Just take a moment to imagine that Jesus was tempted in all manner of human temptations, but was without sin.[17]

What do you believe is the purpose of having emotions? Which emotions can be utilized in literature or drama created by your world view?

MYSTICAL PRIVATE INVOCATIONS OF ART

When artists write music without giving it text, the music makes imprints into a different part of our brain, the non-lingual part. When fog settles into the forest, our senses become alert. When we dance, the power of movement stirs parts of our mind not associated with language. It is often difficult to describe how a dancing string section in an orchestra, moving all of its bows in rhythmic unison, adds to the sound of the concert. How does a careening drum ensemble make a heart leap? Why does a child need to jump and fling her arms in order to make a report about her day at school? It is difficult to find only words to compliment an artist in response to a painting, when what you really want to do is sing it.

Besides all this, every person experiences art with an individual frame of mind, a unique body, a certain context framed in their biology and history. What happens responsively in one soul is not the same thing that happens inside another.

Abstract art speaks to one, while another person appraises the work of impressionism, and still another audience relays the wonder of dark realism.

It is the job of a journalist or art critic to find nuances in language to manipulate expressions that make sense to a broad audience. Crafted through connotation, empirical data, grammar, and figures of speech, typed columns are aimed like arrows, when the work is done, to show respect owed to the artist and to allure new audiences to the art form.

Applause, tears, murmurs or exclamations, and other physical responses are perhaps the most sacred and appropriate immediate results of experiential art and music. This is what God did when he spoke nature into existence with light, and sound and seasons. He authorized from the highest heights, "Ah... HOW GOOD IT IS!"

Who knows all of God's purposes? We may never "get" all the angles of His art. Perhaps when we mimic His creation, our best communication is that we return to Him the compliment of a child's adoration. Some art is reserved for the resonance and confidentiality of God's own heart. No one else may see!

Other times, we offer bits of our childlike awe—some aspect of science or policy or love—as a window to God's world. This fallen world needs windows open to God's wonders. "Let the children come to Me," He calls, inviting through the windows. He is the Potter. We are the clay. The pot doesn't test its maker by challenging, "Why have you made me this way?"[18] Someone looking into your clay pot may see a window opening to wonder. We cannot possibly know all of His reasons for creating.

Rule 4: USE THE LANGUAGE OF YOUR AUDIENCE TO COMMUNICATE your message. Creativity is a gift to you from the Creator. It's for you to use. But listen and taste, then prepare the feast adding in your own flavors and rhythms.

5

MIMIC TRUTH IN MEASURED BREATHS

By taking measured breaths, you enter into an unconscious rhythm.

Inhale. Process life. Exhale. A pulmonary system, as wonderfully complex as it is, takes in a measure of air, then expels it. Lungs have specific physical limits. Their purpose is a primary function to give life to a body. Creatives, too, find a rhythm to life and art that feels natural and works if they are turning out regular art. JUST BREATHE.

A shivoo of great fun is made from the infusion of divine gifts, including what comes naturally to you. Exalt in how God made you to be. Then, exhale your personal process like a natural breath.

Why not draft out an idea? Most visual artists don't start on a big canvas without doing countless thumbnail sketches or a storyboard. You will need to work the angles, add the detail, decide on voicing, sounds, lighting, and smells to make your craft well.

START. Practice breathing your art in natural boundaries. Mimicking the Creator means you accept your starting point and just start breathing, announcing, and working. If you are a novice, you accept that your excitement for your creativity doesn't equate to the skill of a master. Step by step, you come into your own voice, and that voice may change as you grow. Creatives continue to do new things, untried things within certain boundaries of discipline. We become novices daily, intentionally. Being willing to follow Christ and the Holy Spirit into creativity, is the opposite of being "full of ourselves". It is being willing to be renewed daily.

SCOPE. Expressing your place within whole truth is God's good news. An author or artist can provide impressions, shades of images, and likenesses of the Logos, that offer more than a linear process and assessment. The creative's message may haunt someone who doesn't quite get it. Does this sound familiar? "And with that [Jesus] *breathed* on them and said, 'Receive the Holy Spirit.'"[1] Here we see a second opportunity for *those who followed the Christ* to receive a personal relationship to God, to once again be able to walk in peace on the Earth with Him, and even more than that, to forgive sins on His behalf. Where once the Holy Spirit had left the Earth due to holiness separating from sinfulness, here Jesus was offering His precious and powerful transponder, in person, to all *those who chose to make Him their LORD.*

An individual, however, has certain blinders—a

limited reach—a scope of jurisdiction for a purpose. The reach of one soul rises exponentially when individuals work together in teams. Lungs work best when carried on legs, pumped by the movement of arms, feet, and heart, ordered by a mind. Inspiration given to these organs is from the Creator-Christ, and the Holy Spirit moves us forward.

Take inventory.

What is the breadth of your purpose at this time? What tools prop you up?

Who are your teammates?

STRIDE. If you walk a circumference of your landscape to survey boundaries, you'll discover not only new details of your land, but also the costs and benefits of your purpose on it. You may see that you can throw a stone across the skin of a pond on your land, and you'll see that your influence causes ripples. You'll recognize these characteristics and limits as being your platform, your viewpoint, and your scope of expression. Should you research and experiment with your findings—you'll begin to stride around the landscape like only an owner knows how.

Some people you reach with your message will want to hear or see just enough of it to decide whether they agree or approve of the message. Yet, a creative can offer a message to transform a soul and transcend judgments when in stride.

In wrestling with the images, a reader or listener is forced to consider details on the landscape not noticed prior to your message. Be honest against the slippery slope of propaganda for the masses. Be sure to take in enough Spirit, as you breathe deeply, and stride around your landscape seeing new detail. Don't fail to measure the circumference of a structure on your landscape, note the height and interior volumes of space, budget accurately for the cost of building its systems.

You seek a measure of meaning for your landscape design as purposed before time for you and your good work by the Logos.

SPEAK. If you are a Biblical pastor and you decide to enlist in this creativity movement of God, when you breathe in the whole breath of God as He dispenses, you may find yourself breathing a little differently by taking in, processing, and exhaling the story of Sheerah, who became the first female civil engineer and who saved her family's honor in 1 Chronicles 7:24.

Sheerah built Lower and Upper Beth Horon as well as Uzzen Sheerah. You'll preach this image even if some don't like it because it doesn't end with an altar call or because it exalts a woman.

You will include it in your messages because the authority of our LOGOS dictated this story as a necessary part of God's salvation plan. This is good news for us. You may obey this authority even though you experience strong vibrations of discontent.

You may sculpt figures of the Judge and Warrior Deborah or the Heroine Jael, or present plays on Queen Esther. Each expression in God's history book helps to rescue us and opens our view to form the whole picture.

You may be a teacher who figures out the importance of Zelophehad's five daughters' appeal to Moses. They asked to be able to inherit their father's land. You may teach about the wisdom in what God did for women's rights to land and independence, yet also the equitable division of land relating to the rights of the tribes.[2]

Your Biblical theology may include a new poetic turn of phrase, "Now faith is the subject of things hoped for, the evidence of things unseen."[3] There are many realities and so many truths that are unseen. The brain may be viewed and handled, but the mind is illusive. Hands may caress, but the feelings of caresses are not seen. A book is a tangible value because of the intangible word crafted by authors and editors, collected by the symbols of language, and printed by ink and machines onto several pages, cleverly presented by the ingenuity of graphic designers and publishers.

GOOD NEWS IN THE LAW

After people were getting things wrong for some time and finding themselves enslaved, God freed His people from slavery and then penned His expression of succinct law on tablets of stone for preserving the rest and peace of His people. God's Law is part of His God-breathed creative expression for broad, global love. God's glory was also revealed at Mount Sinai when He gave the Law to Moses.[4] Take another look at the LORD's laws for community. Can you inhale the love of King David for the exquisite thoughtfulness of God's law?

We are commanded to set God's law on our foreheads. This command, hyperbole as the image of the Hebrew language implies, instructs us to pin His commandments into our frontal lobes. Why? Our frontal lobe contains most of the dopamine-sensitive neurons in the cerebral cortex. The dopamine system is associated with reward, attention, short-term memory tasks, planning, transcendence, and motivation. Meditate on your Creator's commands in the night. Incorporate them when you are talking about life with others. Talk about them when waking up or when walking along the road. Discuss them and recite the statutes as you mentor your own children who will soon face life's opportunities.[5]

When you speak of Christian artistry, does the "good news" refer only to the cross and resurrection or does "good news" refer to all of God's message?

We have so many mishandled theologies of human nature, God's nature, and a mess of *bumfuzzeled* grace and *canoodled* forgiveness surrounding us. Neither ignorance of our bodies, avoidance of human physiology or omissions of society's need for God's law can be dismissed as inconsequential grace. We have to address these issues in our storytelling and art.

Treating forgiveness without the process of repentance or the evidence of faith may appear creative and appealing, but it is false news. How do you illustrate false belief systems in your plotlines? "Do not conform to the pattern of this world, but be transformed by the renewing of your mind. Then you will be able to test and approve what God's will is—his good, pleasing and perfect will."[6]

Be careful to think things through in order to follow God's Word as it guides your personal creativity. Let it cleanse your own mind of preconceived ideas.

GOOD NEWS IN MARGINS

Margins on a page of a screenplay or theatrical script are an awful lot like the space between notes in a notated song. They are breathing points. They give the brain room to organize, reflect, and rest.

Margins define the positive input of sound, expression, and tonal quality, adding character and descriptive settings for lyrical conversations. Margins allow the reader and listener to add his or her own perspective and experience into the interpretation. The term, "Selah," in the Psalms was a musical indication to pause and reflect.

Margins and boundaries rely on each other for definition.

Ignatius of Loyola readily engaged in dueling to the death with those who denied the divinity of Christ. It wasn't until his legs were broken by a cannon ball, and surgery was conducted without anesthetics, that he came to experience Christ personally. While healing, he read

Di Vita Christi by Ludolf of Saxony. This book proposed that the reader imagine himself or herself in the Gospel settings. Practicing this spiritual exercise transformed Ignatius. So much so, that he hung up his sword and dagger to become disciplined and educated. Finally, he wrote his "Spiritual Exercises" based on the power of transitional meditation. His motto became "For the greater glory of God."[7] Artists, whether practicing in secular fields or religious orders, know the need to rest.

Rest is a holy discipline, and it is wholly important as the active content. In this spirit of rest, an artist receives inspiration, then indicates rather than dictates. No creative earns that god-like power to dictate or bully his or her values and behaviors onto others, but taken in stride, an artist can model and indicate something of value, let it potentially move souls. An artist rests, knowing the Lord will do what He wills in each life.

To covet God's sovereign dictation and His glory for our image or success is to become like Satan rather than God. The twisted result of self-importance is to experience the removal of God's glory. Ignatius of Loyola learned the difference. Clearly, the results of his former life were quite different from that of his latter course.

I would have enjoyed watching how Jesus' disciples eventually learned to work together. Imagine the people Jesus called to His inner circle. John, the disciple whom Jesus loved, was a mystic. Nicodemus and Joseph of Arimathea were pharisees, Paul was a pharisee, Matthew was a publican tax collector, and Simon was a Zealot whose aim it was to unhinge Roman rule. Then, there were the fishermen.

Creatives and pragmatists do well to understand personal boundaries. We wait. We leave margins for God's own voice and use a) through others and b) through other means c) without undercutting another worker. What we don't express may be just as important as what we do express. For example, books don't sell if all their words run together without punctuation, lines off the page, without margins or boundaries.

GOOD IN POLITICS

"Everything is politics," said Thomas Mann.[8] Politics are social constructs in which we all must live. In a heated political economy, the Christian artist can create space and ambient ideas to stimulate new avenues of conversation.

If you have something to say, and a profound means to say it in the proper context and time, you should enter your works into the debates of guns, power, elitism, forgiveness, border walls, the laws of medical care, and the economy of aliens. Use it by the grace of God. To do so may pigeon-hole your future as an artist. Be prepared to follow the Lord. Does your art mimic God's mind and heart with reasoning? Or, is your desire to influence others for *your* laurels, or the pocketbook of a politician's claim on you? Are you being pressured by an altar of agendas prone to explode?

I was raised in a compelling political environment. Yet, the works of artists have provided movement from my first inclination into more life-giving forms of human involvement. Creative works have added merciful legal interventions to my way of thinking and redemptive answers to complex issues. It is these creative connections which have provided truer and more Biblical positions than my earlier viewpoints.

Anyone can be critical, especially about politics. Very few can offer creative solutions. Anyone can become a critical alarmist. It takes someone with goodwill and inspiration to not take aim at the target some wear on their foreheads, but rather understand the higher aim, helping to make rough places straight.

So what if you "hate this administration." Now everyone knows where you stand in the mob, but people cannot respect you for where you walk if you are not moving forward. Who do you follow? Where do you lead others? Are you exemplifying steps to change? To answers? To peace? To God?

I thank God for giving artists voices, and myself ears to hear, in order to consider both sides of the coin and other options for serious dilemmas. My God's margins in my life have been enlarged, but also my borders expanded.

How do we breathe deeply and exhale reason by the Word of Christ? We know that Jesus Christ means "The Help of Jehovah or God's anointed Savior," but how do we invoke God's help to express His intangible reason in our lives? Let's start with a defining question; what is the Word of Christ? What if we can breathe in the Word by absorbing Christ's Own living Spirit, His Holy Spirit?

Something about breathing seems essentially life-giving, enigmatic. It is honest. Just breathing carries its own cross. Life is hard. It barks where it finds a virus, coughing up what ails us. It is in these situations that God's expressions transcend circumstance and shine the brightest. Do we change quotes to gloss over honesty when the outcome seems incomprehensible? His answers pry deeply, haunting our souls. People are looking for authentic versions of God's attributes in the characters and artistic expressions put on display. Don't mimic sappy. Don't be monotonous either! Contrasts are so important. Speak the depth of the matter from a unique context. It is not an aim of mine to wind up a *fopdoodle* of history. Does this appeal to you? Create your story in layers of truth to please God.

The static character of evil is a constant reality that writers can utilize. A good example of a static character is Cinderella's stepmother.[9] A static character is a character in literature or drama who undergoes few changes throughout the duration of the story.

Emie, in the story of *The Whispering of The Willows*, is a fourteen-year-old girl saddled with dysfunctional parents, poverty, betrayal, and the hypocrisy of a preacher.[10] These evils are static characters in the story. Though she and other characters in the book are moving, Emie's "hero" needs to be several people in the community because no one person can rescue a girl from such a situation.

The Whispering of The Willows offers us a model of

how individuals work together in a community to secure a difference in one life.

The Americana memoir, *Mister B*, is the story of a 97-year-old agnostic rocket scientist who rescues a floundering and recalcitrant cook and chauffeur from bankruptcy. Mutual bitterness is transformed in minute measurements, by flutters of humor, as they learn to appreciate *Mister B*'s stories of science, math, international politics, and social history. Answers are not always easy, yet they are transforming.[11]

If you feel like the person of Jesus is a flat story image, a thing of the past, irrelevant to you, try seeing Him as the God of mathematics or science.

One day, my linguist friend, Iris, sat in the seat next to a Dartmouth astronomy professor on an airplane flight. He saw the strange Greek symbols she was working with on her computer and asked about the language she was translating. She explained to him, "the Word doesn't eliminate science by asking people to believe without facts or history. It simply focuses on answering the Why's rather than the How's." The How's are reserved for formula thinkers; so long as we have more to learn, we will never be rid of the need for formulaic thinkers, scientists, linguists, and mathematicians. And, because the questions are unending, we will always have the mystics.

If you feel like the person of Jesus is a flat story image, a thing of the past, irrelevant to you, try seeing Him as the God of the Psalms. *The Word of Christ is contained in the Old Testament not only through nature, but also through the foreshadowing of sacrifice, holiness, the king's marriage psalm, adoption, redemption, and victory and judgment.* Why does the New Testament direct modern Christians to sing the old Psalms?

Christ may not be mentioned in the book of Psalms, but Christ embodies all the expression and Personhood of God. So, worshippers may need to think backward to get the full impact of who Christ is in the meditations of the Psalms. We contemplate Jesus in error if we contemplate Him as any less terrifying than the Father from the mortal perspective, or any more compassionate or full of grace. He is the fulfillment of the law, and He is so much more than that.

The disciple whom Jesus loved best quotes Jesus, claiming, "If anyone is thirsty, let him come to me and drink, and out of his heart will flow streams of living water."[12] If we can nurture children and teenagers toward the disciplines of God's word, teaching them to seek the LORD and obey Him during the developmental stages of life, then streams of living water will flow out of their core toward others. It's a promise.

Living water is the sweetest metaphor for a flow of life-giving words.

When we mull over God's Word to us with friends, or sing the Psalms together, we carry the expressions of God for ourselves and for others on our breath, like drops and sprays of living water. Breath that would normally be a pulmonary exercise for personal benefit, now carries God's Word. It, then, is breathing out a gift of life for others in addition to simply breathing for our own good.

WRESTLING WITH LIMITS

In our writing group, we have often used limiting exercises to see what can be written. These have included writing a page without the use of a vowel, writing a story only in diphthongs, writing a poem of homonyms, or filling in the story when given an opening sentence and a closing statement. What a fun reward to hear the variety of creative expressions that come of these limiting exercises.

If creativity meant that there were no limits, when God said, "make the ark this many cubits, with wood that can withstand and float in this kind of water and wind,"[13]— what if Noah had said, "Nope! This other kind of wood is prettier and I want to save some of it for retrofitting and woodworking after the flood... I want to be creative as an individual in my own right to see what happens." Or, "I prefer to work in broad strokes rather than following the exact mathematics and building codes. Yes, the codes are given for the purpose of safely housing a host of animals and people needing food storage during long days of depressing rain without sight of land, but I'd rather not." The alternative is irony!

God's Law is not legalism. The real purpose of the Law of God is to keep us all safe and creatively free.

The ten commandments were set down for an important and good purpose. Liberty! "Because I brought you out of bondage, therefore..."[14]. they are God's expression of goodness, mercy, and justice toward a whole community. There are rules of fashion, rules for social media, rules of politics and economics. Why, then, do we buck against spiritual rules for success? But, stories of our misunderstandings, wanderings and sins make for our own authentic stories of walking to glory. When our boundaries are our circumstances and the laws of God are accepted as good benefits for others, we are suddenly forced into creativity because we cannot indulge our natural bent toward tit-for-tat or indulge in self-pity.

Depict the difference. When you don't commit adultery, steal or murder, or extort the powerless, you can build up others.

Southern author, Flannery O'Connor, wove the threads of her stories in the value of common sense and foolhardy humanity. Like a modern Aesop, she removed any lingering romance from the wiles of wicked men.

Maybe it was the cackle of her peacocks, which she kept on her property, that provided her the courage to write such tales. Maybe it was the annoying fact that only the male peacock is costumed in exquisite feathers for strutting. Maybe it was being housebound.[15]

O'Connor's creativity caused me to look again at the goodness of staying close to the laws of God and far away from the pride of life, lusts of the flesh, and the deceitfulness of being polite to coyotes.

When creatives wrestle with depraved circumstances and overarching laws of God, they can come up with some deeply moving stories, which, as Helena Sorenson states, do not provide a reader an escape from reality, but offers a reader an escape into reality. She stated in a

Rabbit Room podcast, The Artist's Creed, April 9, 2019, hosted by Steve Gutherie of Belmont University, that believers live in two realities, and that when our white noise tracks and rules are removed, the new rules of fantasy enable us to see the spiritual realities through new windows. Read the book of Jonah and take a good look at God's darkly comical perspective for His aberrant servant. Read the story of Sampson's passion for the Philistine girl in light of Judges 14:4, where it states, "His father and mother didn't realize the LORD was at work in this, creating an opportunity to work against the Philistines, who ruled over Israel at that time" (NLT).

It is a crime, in my opinion, to create dishonest art, even if the dishonesty is an attempt to clean up doctrine.

The purpose of parody, irony, and fantasy is not to hide the truth, but to expose it. If you are going to deal in the art of good news, deal honestly with bad news. Limits compel us to get creative. Limits provide detail and wonderful margins for curiosity.

PIERCING THE VEIL

Is the creative expression of God always determined by whether a clear conversion to Christ is depicted and witnessed by the reader within the confines of a story? Since all the world belongs to Him, may we depict other stories so desperate as to haunt a reader forever, leaving the outcome to God?

"Last night, Paul and I were quite frustrated with Mister B's anxiety over a new nurse coming to bathe him.

He shouted at the nurse, 'Go away! Leave me alone!' He insisted, 'I can take care of myself.' He's 102 years old.

'Okay, then, Mister B. We'll just close the door and let you do it. We'll be right here if you need us.' Ten minutes later when there is no sound of water or movement, I peek in the door. He is sitting on the edge of his bed fully dressed.

"'Mister B, you said you were taking a shower! You are stinky, you can't come downstairs without one.'

"'I'm not sick. I didn't say I would take a shower. I want the freedom to make my own choices, and live the way I want to live, stinky or not!'

"I tried to cajole him, reason with him that he needs help, but he moaned that he'd rather die than have a nurse watching him bathe naked. He turned back into bed and lay down.

"The nurse left.

"All day, Mister B preferred to stay in bed and ignore the world rather than to get cleaned up. Finally, coming out of his shell for dinner, he ate a good full plate of food, and just when we were getting comfy in our respective after-dinner chairs, he requested a shower from Paul. 'Would you have the time to give me a shower tonight, and get that out of the way?' he said.

"Paul, so good-hearted and more compassionate than his frustrated wife, did just that. Up the stairs they went, 'Good-night.' 'Good-night.'

"Down the stairs came Paul fifteen minutes later to have a moment in the back yard garden with me and his cigar.

"'YOU are a good man, honey,' I said.

"'It's nothing,' he said. But, I know that my husband

is quite something! It's so much more work for him to come home from the hospital only to do a bath for his dad when he was fully prepared to relax in his easy chair after dinner.

"After Paul's smoke curls up into the sky and evaporates with the day, we head up to an early bedtime ourselves. He peeks into Mister B's bedroom. His dad is reaching up to the ceiling with an arm, and waving it back and forth.

"'Whatcha doing, Chief?' Paul asks.

"'I'm just feeling the freedom of exercising my arm.'"

—Author Lynn Byk[16]

> **Does God's good news always rush to the resurrection of Jesus, or does He also want us to know that he sits with His children in corners of their confusion and identifies with human poverty and abuse?**

In Matthew Chapter 4, we have the story of the devil tempting Jesus, who is hungry and tired. Satan demands that He use his powers to turn stones into food. Jesus answers, "Man shall not live by bread alone, but by every word that proceeds from the mouth of God."[17] One of the obvious messages in this passage is that food isn't enough to sustain life. Yet, this passage and Jesus' answer has always haunted me. What is really happening here besides Jesus' hunger? What has He been up to for these forty days besides spending intense time in fellowship with His Father?

This story is not a story of salvation, per se. Yet, it is so valuable that it is included in the accounts of Jesus' life, even though so few of us can hope to decipher it's meaning. Personal stories matter to God, even if no one else understands.

Now that you understand more of the expansive depth, width, and breadth of being in relationship with God's creative LOGOS, can you imagine that part of your calling is to write, model, or make personal art about your relationship with God?

Jesus had just been anointed for ministry, according to this Matthew passage, chronicling His personal temptations. He was in deep fellowship with His Father. This time of intimacy caused Jesus to choose His Father's companionship over food and physical nourishment. He knew His Father would take care of Him.

In this passage, Jesus knows His scripture. He quotes it back to Satan as a defense.

Does exhaling the Word of God always specifically pertain to God's written word of stories, statutes and the ordained judgments of God—to quoting verses of Scripture—or is there more to copying the Creator than just using scriptural language? I believe that Jesus used scripture against Satan because Satan was subject to its power. Besides that, Satan had no idea what Jesus was experiencing with God, and Jesus had no duty or inclination to inform him about it.

The canvas of the creative's praise and worship is larger than one can possibly imagine or fill in a lifetime! God's creativity and unending inspiration is a canvas for the entire universe! The canvas is also deeply personal, and as such, quite small.

Understanding the context now, what does this phrase include for you: *Every word that proceeds from the mouth of God*?

Near the conclusion of Anne Lamott's book, *Hallelujah Anyway*, she describes holding onto sobriety, sinking into a church bench to which she had tethered herself, as itinerate preachers filled the pulpit. She, the newcomer to Christianity, taps her foot in the pew waiting for some word of wonder to break from the droning speaker. "I still remember. . . that I stayed, *uncomfortable* and understanding next to nothing, until I heard the words I needed. But the choir fed me until then. Their voices were like a life raft in choppy waters, and the lightweight boat held me and the harmonies of words I couldn't make sense of gave voice to a beauty inside me, which I could not yet access, and could not possibly have made by myself."[18]

Experiment with the power of our senses, with a jolt or fresh juice in your tale. If the only symbol or image you use in your writing is the cross, people will peg you and assume they already know your subject matter, and where you are going with it. Surprise your audience. If you only want to write on the theme of redemption, try using the same divine experiment under different conditions. Use different time frames, different characters in your world or imagination, different temptations, different twists. Dare to push your story beyond the expected. Trust that maximal themes will emerge in one of the drafts.

One of the writers in my writer's group early on introduced me to the short stories of Ray Bradbury. Characterized as Fantasy Literature and Horror Fiction, I wasn't sure about the discomfort of walking in Mr. Bradbury's lumpy old shoes. In the end, he, along with Flannery O'Connor, became two good, leather boots in forming purpose and protecting my ideas of godly imagination. Godly writing does not necessarily have to tie up all of the loose ends.

Adam's grandson, Jubal, became the father of all those who play the lyre and pipe. His other grandson, Tubal-cain, became the forger of all implements of bronze and iron.[19] Many years, many stories, many wars, many legacies, many twists-and-turns passed before Jesus was born. Some hauntingly wide berths of margin, where wonder and rest become the ingenious endings to a compelling argument.

Because God is infinite, neither He nor His purposes can ever be completely revealed. Philosopher Karl Barth wondered aloud how the Omnipresence of God possibly became a here-and-now being. Through Mary the Mother of God, the divine Jesus became part of the human race.[20]

Your impressions of the good news in made up stories may feel like improvisations, but prayerfully consider bringing them to life.

Rule 5: MEASURE YOUR ACTS TO FIND YOUR PLACE IN THE SCOPE OF THINGS. Open up. Improvise. Get 'er flying. Sing, shout, or whisper. Practice using your own story to find where it matters.

6

FOCUS ON DETAIL

When I was in one of my creative cycles, trying to figure out my artistic future, things were happening to me. *Not very nice things.* By people in my family and by my surrounding neighbors. At first, I thought what had happened in my family was the worst-possible thing that could ever happen. Then, the day after our Christian hospitality house received its seal of occupancy, my neighbors started stalking us. They didn't approve of our home or of us using our home for hospitality, so they stirred up zoning laws, building citations, and a consecutive series of lawsuits. We were as likely to have a missionary staying in our guest suite while on furlough, as a policeman at the door handing over another citation.

When you are misunderstood by even one person in your world, it can set your day off-balance. It can reach into a week like a bad flu, or take over a month with self-questioning; even years of debilitating rearrangements of your well-purposed life could be required depending upon how long the misunderstanding goes, and how like a poison branch dropped into the well, it might spread.

At first, I behaved well. I put my head down. I smiled back. I prayed for the oppressors. I tried to figure out ways to bless them. All my building designs had been signed off by an engineer and an architect and the city departments. Why couldn't the neighbors leave us be?

Then, I began to shine the light onto the bad behavior and ask questions that I hoped would lead back to the truth. But, my question-asking became a form of mockery about those on the other side of the wall. It was clever mockery, so people on my side gave me pleasing reactions.

Our quiet Christian hospitality home gained a reputation because of my slightly naughty questions and political analysis of what was going on. When the municipal court sent me complaints, I answered them as best I could. All the time, I was hoping people would use common sense and be neighborly. I kept asking for help from the Christian legal community and got nowhere. Having defended myself, the best legal strategy for the defense had become muddied and complicated.

Nearing the end of six years of miserable struggle, our church asked me whether I would give an Easter testimony about victory in Christ for the Palm Sunday message. Anger welled up and spilled over for the feelings of helplessness, isolation, fear, betrayal, and my own reactions to the assaults we had endured as a family and household.

Add the irony of the Easter testimony request to our situation, and I fell into a deep depression. A vision of Jesus Christ came to me in that state. He was sitting in sackcloth, half-naked in a mud puddle next to me. I was weeping and saying sorry for the way that I'd dragged His name through the mud and horse crap. That's how I felt about it.

Jesus was scrawny. His face and body were smeared with whatever we were sitting in. He turned to me, and smiled gently, but there was a noticeable missing tooth. My stomach tensed with mortification and grief.

He said to me, "You can't do anything worse to me than what has already been done. I'm going to sit here with you as long as it takes." And, that was the testimony I gave. Sometimes the miracle of Christ is that He will sit with us in mortification. *As long as it takes.*

That moment revealed that we too often rush through the Passover night of betrayal and the excruciating fake trials Jesus endured, being flogged, and carrying his cross on the road to Golgotha. The horrid hours of Jesus' prolonged death are swept under the rug in favor of the resurrection platform, for we are the recipients of salvation because Jesus conquered death.

In my suffering, I learned to focus on details I hadn't seen before. To me, focusing on the hours and years of my own betrayal, my own demise, while trying to rise above the slander and libel, gave me insight into the injustice others experience, and what damage mass mentality, even of Christians, can do.

Funny enough, I experienced a deep sense of wanting to defend the feelings of God! His own betrayal and the way He was, and still is, mocked and cursed and misrepresented, must feel horrible!

Within a year of this Easter experience, my old life was buried, and I found myself entering a new business.

Being Creative

In 2014, traditional publishing houses were experiencing a crisis. Publishers like Kindle, CreateSpace, and Smashwords, began selling books to the public directly, books at low cost. The "big five" publishers absorbed smaller houses. Would-be authors recognized that all of the traditional publishers ignored any query letter that was not from a well-connected author or a person with a well-established contact list and a public platform base.

Brick and mortar retailers swept their shelves and closed doors. Rookie authors could not get signed on, yet they yearned to offer their own books to the public. They didn't understand how dire it was to have professional editors rake over their work. They didn't know where to find these ethereal editors or how to find cover designers, formatters, and book distributers.

Capture Books filled a niche. Personally though, an array of deficits plague me. It was a sad conglomeration of deficits. Never very good at detail, I'm a big picture person, a collaborator, and a lover of good literature. I'm a tenacious servant, but homonyms, grammar, and punctuation are not my strong suit. To solve these problems, I hired a relay of editors to do that work.

Case in point, Auralee Arkinsly's early-reader chapter book, *Darling Hedgehog Goes Down a Foxhole*, was released in ARC form.[1] Burgeoning with glorious illustrations and lovely prose, we were so pleased. After our author Kathy Joy read it, she contacted me and said, "Has anyone caught the incorrect use of the term peddle on page 11?" The light of Sunday morning drained away.

We'd missed something. A homophone. The correct word was not implemented, and the cost to our company was not only financial, but a cost to our publishing reputation.

We were already touting the book for teaching second grade simile, why not include all three homophones: pedal (peddling a bicycle with feet to the pedals), petal (through a rose petal path), to peddle mushrooms in town? That, we did.

When you focus on detail, you gain insight. You earn authority. You practice accurate observation skills. You gain inspiration. This is the good work of a creative person. When you focus on detail, you recognize a wrong turn. You do your homework, though homework is hard. Check and recheck. Submit to editors. Submit to proofreaders. Write. Rewrite.

Mimicking the Creator doesn't mean you avoid points of controversy or grotesque detail. You don't avoid word pictures of the voiceless, abandoned, abused, or extorted. You don't avoid what you fear the most. You don't gloss over hatred and murder. Instead, you determine to hunt down and tackle these details with names and complex situations. In the book of Judges, there is a story reported as horrific as Dateline, Evil, or Criminal Minds. The briefest detail relays that a man chopped up his concubine and sent pieces of her to all the tribes of Israel.[2] This psychological drama pointed to the mentality of the men of a certain city. The details sent by courier raised such ire that the deed was exposed and the men were indicted with proof of their abuse for punishment. Those tales are in Scripture for a purpose. They make us ask about human character and God's character. Authors and script writers do not have to be "clean" or "safe" to write with a Biblical worldview.

If you only retell safe stories, or retell well-known Bible characters' stories, your own stories may be sacrificed. The real teaching opportunity for what God is doing in today's world through you, may be lost. Without self-examination, bringing home current life applications may be missed. How does it feel to put one's own brother into the scene? Creativity ignites the mind, but detail and well-executed form tugs at the emotions. We often call this experience "wonder." As my nephew, Elliott, said, "Emotions are energy forces. Emotions may arise from one situation and be transferred in their complexity into another journey, gaining new benefits, new applications to spring modern traps."

Does your scary story help the reader wonder how the Holy Spirit would lead you through a dilemma if you were put into a situation of violence or entrapment? A lightning strike of emotion, a natural reaction, will inform a writer of how the Creator feels about the situation. Our emotions mirror His.

Emotions have limits, however, and can be manipulated by storytellers for perverse agendas. Though it haunts you, emotion itself just isn't your lodestar. Emotional situations make you wonder about yourself, about life, about strategy, timing, and creative solutions. These details lead us to the truth, but we harness our feelings to serve truth, not to believe all that our emotions tell us blindly.

Using a broad berth of emotional power in your writing, however, can fuel the next step. Focus on using feelings to release faithful inspiration or transformation.

The Logos of the person of Christ is that He is the best form of God to our eyes, like a business logo. When we create a character in our stories, we develop tell-tale logos of their personality or character. If the character is nervous, worried, or improperly healed, give them a physical tic like an involuntary finger movement. A very kind woman may be revealed by scenes at a hospital or a dog rescue, but she draws the line of compassion every time she interacts with her mother because of injury sustained by her. Santa is always depicted with a twinkle in his eye. Certain characters must dress in the fine fashion of Paris, while others dress in flannel or woolen shirts and still others dress in detailed futuristic outfits. Adding each detail, a favorite meal, a missing tooth, a pan on the head, a historic colloquialism, an accent, or manner of speech, is to create the logo—the representation of each character.

Artistic people love to portray the nuances of human experience and dislike pat answers and religious gimmicks in commerce. Christian artists love to discover the truth in the complexity of life, but are often shy to iterate it inside their own books. Christian biases do censor by denominations and by personal chagrin. But when an author performs the research in real world data and in Scripture, the story details are set for emotional impact. God will be true. His promises will yield rewards.

We long to dive for our own pearls hidden in oyster shells of the deep, to copy real pearls with synthetic processes as best we can, and to express some sense of value in our own unique way. In fiction, this is best achieved by detailing pockets of realism and psychological paths to suspend disbelief. In faith, we write about many aspects of humanity coinciding with revelations of God.

During the hours spent calculating the odds of taking a terrifying risk, or standing with your nose in the corner, or using a ruler that is too short to measure the material, these pockets provide a context in which you develop new ways of thinking. Lazy work will be sent back to the writer and may never be published. Writers need to search the Word of God personally to allow it to light up their corners, light up where a path will lead, and show the stumbling stones which can be used to develop a character or distract or trick the reader in a mystery.

You may give a classroom of writers the story context of Joseph's crucible, that of being betrayed by his siblings,[3] and ask them to write a story about it. They will have to wrestle with their own temptations for retribution, jealousy, or isolation, being falsely blamed, and overlooked. They will learn to tune into their own humanity and track God's involvement in their own story.

You may want to point writers to one of the dilemmas between Cain and Abel,[4] or Abraham and Lot,[5] or Moses, who chose to identify with the children of Israel rather than with Pharaoh's daughter and her culture of wealth and advantage.[6] Moses had a choice between mothers.

Setting up a character's mannerisms, names, vocal idiosyncrasies, use of clothing, food preferences, height, weight, toys, and political idioms, helps the audience sense when and where things go awry. There may be a physiological twist related to these details as the struggle begins—a struggle that is only disclosed later. A pertinent detail in the backstory may come to light as the story resolves. A creative person likes to search out the details because the details turn on lights, sounds, and odors. Adding descriptive details such as an olfactory memory or a musical psychosis to a series of scenes, helps the audience enter into a person's fear with comprehension.

Ecclesiastes 12:10–13 says, "The Preacher sought to find delightful words and to write words of truth correctly. The words of wise men are like goads, and masters of these collections are like well-driven nails; they are given by one Shepherd. [...] The conclusion, when all has been heard, is: fear God and keep His commandments because this applies to every person..." (NASB).

Many, many manuscripts are written. . .

It's the book with the lucid logic, clever observations, and a set of details which makes the difference. Do your characters' voices have a secret habit? Where does it come from? Do they mumble something repeatedly? Are they from a sub-culture? What was the landmark in a character's life which allows he or she to proceed in your story the way you want to write it? Does your plot contain both logic and surprise?

If you are a painter or photographer, you must pay attention to the chemicals in the colors and the characteristics of the paper. If you are an engineer or architect, you must understand the quality and characteristics of the materials being used, the thickness of them and the powers of outside wind shear. If you are a performer, you must obey the rules of left stage, right entrances and exits, vocalization techniques, and of body mechanics protecting your physical carriage. The message properly conducted to the audience without interruption. A stage is taped with an "X" for a reason. Voices break down. It isn't wise to gloss over the detail.

If your manuscript has holes, look to see whether delight, truth, and end results show a reverence for God's Law and Grace. Spinners of news items know that using an understatement can evoke public mockery and even curse something that was worthy of reward. Word choice or phrasing, a misuse of a term, or a new application of an idea, can color the meaning of what was originally intended. This is how we get *fake news*. Slander, libel, and gossip. Inserting details can be used for good or for evil. Have you ever read someone's take on an essay or book and before reading it yourself, you believe the critique and pass it along only to discover that your opinion differs significantly when you honestly take the time to indulge in the material? Conveying details true or skewed wields immediate power, sometimes to a fault.

On the other side of bringing accuracy to light for the purpose of breeding righteousness, stands the recipient.

The recipient is not always interested in the necessity of enlightening minds, especially when the information fails to conform to his or her bias. When a presenter judges a person's actions in a situation, the recipient can dismiss this accuracy using a monstrous filter of "He judged me!" "She attacked me personally!" and, "They shouldn't judge" statements. I particularly love this response: "So, I suck." Meaning, a person is unable to separate one attitude or action from the rest of his or her person.

> List some of the Creator's good work because it is living art. 🎵 Compare this with a list of stationary good works since they are predictable.

Meanwhile, the detailed definitions of the terms "judgment" and "critique" and their proper uses are not pervasively respected. We prefer pats on the back, don't we? Without a respect for knowledge and the ability to be corrected, the people perish in stupid feuds.

In ignorance, we stand unprepared for all the questions life will present to us. Unless we learn from many teachers, we remain silly ostriches who abandon their snugly-nested eggs to wild animals.

We have books, newspapers, magazines, and journals to read and, of course, we have all kinds of media as well: audiobooks, podcasts, movies, athletics, games, billboards, counselors, spouses ignoring, lovers pursuing, friends and passersby, music and measurements.

Only a *Scobblelotcher* avoids the hard work of learning and properly applying knowledge. Sloppiness will leak out of the ears and from orifices meant to produce waste when you are lax. Do your research. Quote facts even if they seem to contradict. Screw the goads into the story line, apply the science. Use the trajectory of a scalpel, state the exact math and strength of the material used in the nail. Follow the evidence.

Be intentional. Choose mentors and entertainment wisely. Fear God in all you read, watch, write, and paint. Keep His commandments even in what you watch, and listen to, and read.[7] Read with the enlightenment of the Holy Spirit and the help of others inside and outside the body of Christ. If you choose not to serve God's built-in, natural warning signs in rest, stewardship, and time management, and in how you create, your body will begin to betray you. Your mind may become soft or twisted. Your muscles may not get the exercise they need. Maybe this is dysphemism, but there will be natural consequences to wasting your time and effort.[8] For many reasons, rivers of *diddly-squat*, i.e., cheap drivel, rises to your ears. Floods of inconsequential entertainment avoid the real detail of character development and a higher calling. Be wise. Seek to uncover shades of deceptions like a plague. The world needs creatives who fear God and who model His commandments as a way to tell the complex tales in the juxtaposition of each character's aims and mishaps.

Returning from the New York Book Expo of 2017, I realized that, more than ever, I wanted to publish

Christian literature appraised as *quality* literature. Not many libraries are stocking the classics with a Christian worldview these days, and modern Christian books can be regarded as sales gimmicks—soft, sentimentalism, unreal, and lacking in quiet observations and wonderful sentences that burn one's lips.

What are literary minds skeptical about? About the honesty and relevance of Christian authors. About a lack of skill in weaving a story. About using art to sell censored conversation, ideas lacking new angles and second-hand regurgitation. They don't want to digest a unilateral sermon dictated on the page. By reading, they want to experience a journey of discovery themselves, a conversation of ideas, some genuine conversion of the author to his or her subjects.

In the oxymoron of the genre called "Christian fiction", our stories are only as deep as the mirror on the wall. Since romance alone does not recreate deeper life dilemmas or character growth, the writer must add a crux of moral dilemma, some dead ends or legal, ethical hard spots. Centrifugal forces add reality to great fictional stories.

Critics don't recommend books that fail to suspend disbelief or that miss purposeful engagement. In life, as in writing, it is important to specify a person's perspective and interests. Pinpoint the one thing that sets each character apart. You may not like it, but don't let your real world fill up with a mishmash of generalities. Describe a plurality of differences. Ping these off the walls, let them waft to the skies—Speak about, exploit, or describe all the variations and differences.

In conversation on December 3, 2019 at the UCLA School of the Arts and Architecture, Ali Behdad said, "The extent to which we all come from different backgrounds and we have different histories, different things matter to each of us. So, for example, for my yoga teacher, what matters is love. For the rich clientele who take his classes at Equinox, what matters is fitness. To our chancellor, probably what matters is public education." He referred to Isaiah Berlin's definition of pluralism, "the recognition that human goals are many, none of them commensurable and in perpetual rivalry with one another." When human values come into conflict, Behdad said, "It doesn't mean that one value is superior to the other one or that it is more true."[9]

What matters is a matter of perspective, and it changes over time. Lisa Beebe reported Ali Behdad talking about growing up in Iran in the '70s: "As a teenager, his belief in freedom of expression, economic equality and social justice inspired him to join street demonstrations, many of which turned violent. When his worried parents prevented him from participating, he was angry, thinking that they didn't care about things like liberty, equality and justice. He said, 'In retrospect, I now appreciate that for them, safety mattered and that their admonitions were coming from a place of love, not cowardice.'"[10]

Weaving both reality and a sense of direction for redemption will provide the most satisfying, detailed story.

When critical readers are not offered the experience of a character's depth of soul in a silent moment, or some twisting, suspenseful circumstance to form the character's future, they fail to experience a deeper reality themselves. "It's just an okay book, nothing special," they'll say. Readers are thirsty for living water from a living source containing images of the Logos at work. When a story fails to hand over this living gift, it entertains on a short stick with a lesser accomplishment. It lacks the broader *A-HA!*

Creatives have to occasionally take stock asking, whose story are we mimicking? Who is mentoring, correcting us? Do we need to focus on a different detail? Let's unveil another aspect of God in the a-ha! journey.

The Christian market also provides a lot of theological sermons, persuasive teachings, and how-to books. The best of these use great literary techniques. They rule their game by taking decisive action on behalf of one side or the other, by storytelling, and by attending to the details required for success. Decide to serve up genuine significance with your work rather than messing around with the *snallygaster.* My prayer is that Christian storytellers and artists create gut-wrenching literature, journeys of stumbling honesty, and new discoveries in God's world. May the LORD make miracles of it.

Rule 6: LOOK CLOSER. Research, list and explore details to enliven your work. Let the details open up unique opportunities.

7

FIND AND EXPLORE SEMIOTIC SURPRISES IN GOD'S EXPRESSIONS

Sometimes you need to start at the end to get a clearer picture of your aims, your personal character arc, your fragment of faith, and who matters. Have you read Mary Oliver's poem, "The Summer Day," which ends with the often-quoted line, "Tell me, what is it you plan to do with your one wild and precious life?"

Careful balance is not always the best aim in life. How would you be able to fully experience the extent of something if you are worried about equilibrium and caution? Think about what you'd want your epitaph to say. Those little quotes are pretty small. There isn't room for many words. Which words will you choose that matter, that will capture the essence of your lodestar or sum up your humanity?

Lovers of literature are looking for surprises. Lovers of life are looking for peace in their community. Rebels are looking for a springboard. All these things signify the demand for meaning. Semiotics is the study of making meaningful communication in specific settings.

Semiotics includes the study of: signs and symbols, signification, logos, signing processes, allegory, analogy, the likeness of images, signage, sign language, metonymy, metaphor, symbolism, significance, and communication.[1]

The powers that oversee book reviews and library content seek new insight from passionate writers and authors with hooks that offer new layers of meaning to lifelike characters and stories. To their credit, they also want to promote awareness of social issues, which is, on the surface, a proselytizing act of literary persuasion similar to evangelical authoring. The form contains inherent danger because the end is a prefabricated aim, so the middle of the tale is hard-pressed not to follow a rote passage of persuasion to a conclusion. The dilemma for a literary critic and for the author is the margin of art versus recognizable prefabrication.

Those who partner with a social or political non-profit, or even a for-profit organization, can force an artist's hand to produce work that is more propaganda than heart-felt art. Art as propaganda promotes a social agenda veiled in a storyline. Because agencies, artists, and publishing houses need a powerbase for funding, they use persuasive art or artists.

Know your artistic philosophy and spiritual pedagogy

> None of us write in a complete void. How do you make note of the subtle turnings of perspective or beliefs that you experience along your own journey in order to draw from them later?

ahead of time to be safe from letting yourself be exploited against your own convictions.

The search for meaning and survival is underlined by the search for surprise and truth. Art can gently cup the breast of one who does not yet recognize his or her longing for love or the need for connection from the Lover of Souls. It can create an eagerness to know and the willingness to wait for further direction.

In the New York Times Bestseller, "Learning to Walk in the Dark," by Barbara Brown Taylor, the argument is laid out that as an Episcopal pastor, she was busy upholding "the way chief Christian teaching thrives on dividing reality into opposed pairs: good/evil, church/world, spirit/flesh, sacred/profane, light/dark. Even if you are not Christian, it should be easy to tell which half of the pair is 'higher' and which half is 'lower.' In every case, the language of opposition works by placing half of reality closer to God and the other half further away."[2]

She shows through prayers and church messages how

Christians can use the theme of darkness ad nauseum to
show evil, wickedness, doubt and fear, yet fail to show
that the Bible also teaches that God created both the day
and night, that He separates both with lights in the sky,
and that He creates seasons of darkness for different
kinds of growth and wonder. "I will give you the
treasures of darkness and riches hidden in secret places,
so that you will know that it is I, the LORD, the God of
Israel, Who calls you by name."3

What a mistress of a well-turned paragraph Barbara
is. Besides finding and exploiting the humor in every
thought for a tah-dah polish, she manages to take us on a
journey under the moon and stars to cast shadows on
where some Christian thought has gone awry and what
we've been missing by not enjoying the literal walk in the
darkness, as well as the spiritual walk.

Her argument is that we too often pray for God to,
"deliver us from powers of darkness. Shine into our
hearts the brightness of Your Holy Spirit, and protect us
from all the perils and dangers of the night." She says,
"Worst of all, [this language] offers people of faith a giant
closet in which they can store everything that threatens
or frightens them without thinking too much about these
things."4 It is this problem which also bothers me.

Because we have a guide in the darkness, as we do in
the light, we are meant to be growing up thinking and
communicating more holistically the older we get, not
continuing to put bandages on disease and darkness.
Holistic means: in a way that is characterized by
comprehension of the parts of something as intimately

interconnected and explicable only by reference to the whole.[5]

When I lived in Africa, I met the site manager of a large youth camp. In the wee hours of the morning, still very much nighttime, it was his practice to awaken his young daughter from sleep, put her onto his shoulders and carry her around the acres hectares as he performed his grounds inspections. When a friend and I were chased, berated, and pecked in broad daylight by a flock of nasty geese, the thought of this three-year-old being out in the cycles of moon with her father among African green mambas, baboons, springbok, and wildebeest felt irresponsible and frightening. I would like to follow up with that grown woman today to know how she feels about these nightly tours with her father.

On December 29, 2015, in a National Public Radio conversation between Hidden Brain podcast host, Shankar Vedantam, and one time Itzek Perlman protégé, Maya Shankar, revealed that damage to her pinky finger and a tendon in her hand brought her musical career and studies at Julliard to an untimely end. "What followed in the days after her musical career ended was an incredible sense of loss.

"'I was really devastated to lose something that I was completely in love with, and so passionate about, and that had really constituted such a large part of my life and my identity,' she says. 'I was first and foremost a violinist.'"

Maya didn't know whether she would ever find another place of belonging and passion in her world. One day she read a story that inspired her to find out more. The interview, From Julliard to the White House, explains how the debilitating loss opened up a way for birthing Maya's new passion. "Today, Maya has reached a new pinnacle in an entirely different field. At the age of 30, she is a senior adviser at the White House working to create better policy using insights from behavioral science. Her work is far-reaching helping students get to college and workers save more for retirement, and millions of children get access to school lunch." She is filled with passion for her new career. [6]

Storytellers, like John Bunyan, who wrote from a prison cell[7], like Annie Dillard, waking up to life in the American Midwest in the 50s[8], and like George MacDonald, who often lost pulpits in Victorian England and Wales due to his conscientious preaching, are examples to us.[9] MacDonald authorized his wife and daughters to take the stage performing Christian dramas as forms of preaching, teaching truth.[10] We need these voices. We need the Brothers Grimm and Aesop's *zounderkites*––ah, those idiots––getting themselves into trouble because they didn't take their characters to heart prior to interacting with them.

If God loves whom He disciplines, then our idiotic experience matters, and each corrective step of insight means something. We can distill these like the essence of lavender oil for healing what ails us.

C.S. Lewis' allegories and storytelling phoenixed from his war training in youth, his classical literature course in college, and from observations of his own spiritual transformation when he encountered true love and then the tragedy of death.[11] G.K. Chesterton's humor and insight were products of self-examination in public life and the study of the Word.[12] Dorothy Sayers' detective mysteries and newspaper journalism were the cloaks in which to hide her private life.[13]

The mystic writers, and others like John Tolkien,[14] Hannah Hunnard,[15] and Madeleine L'Engle,[16] each traveled through major life transitions as they wrote, to survive.

The question is whether we have enough faith to explore the darkness, or do we use all of our faith only to build castles where we can lock our doors and pull all the curtains across our windows?

Learning to walk in the dark is to also recognize the long hours which lay between daylight and darkness and also between darkness and daylight, the time between times. The Celtic people believed these times were mystical and could usher people into different times. Charmayne Hafen, author of the children's chapter book trilogy, "Land of Twilight," exploits that idea in the modern world to lead her protagonist, a wounded child of divorce, into the possibilities of divine hope, friendship, and a walk of faith, though she couches these concepts in Celtic myths.[17]

Barbara Brown Taylor points out, "Once you start realizing how many important things in the Bible happen at night, the list grows quickly."[18] She cites some of God's big promises, and the dreams of saints and wrestlers, also the exodus from Egypt. Beyond that, she reminds us that

God promised to come to Moses not only in the burning bush, but also in a dense cloud of darkness "araphel," because He is merciful.[19] God uses bright light and covers Himself in shrouds of darkness in order to shield people from the reality of His glory, which if shown, could consume us.

The *mysterium tremendumet fascinans* is, "the terrible and fascinating mystery of God which exceeds human ability to manage it in any way [...] Gregory of Nyssa said, 'those of us who wish to draw near to God should not be surprised when our vision goes cloudy, for this is a sign that we are approaching the splendor of God.'"[20]

THE GOOD NEWS IS SCIENTIFIC, PSYCHOLOGICAL, AND MATHEMATICAL NEWS

For Western school teachers, have you wondered how it is that the mathematical system you use to tutor students, which was developed in Asia and the Middle East, *is from the LORD?* How is teaching math or science a Biblical virtue? Yet, you instinctively understand that teaching and applying math and science are good news to simple minds. In your goodwill toward your students, you long for them to excel in these studies.

You long for students to look up the definitions and connotations of words and to understand the broad and adaptive meanings to the things they say and write about. Since our alphabet and rules of grammar were developed in England, were limited by the Midwest, and were broadened by Broadway and Hollywood, how are these tools from the LORD? These things are not necessarily Biblical, but neither is driving a car, turning on the light switch, operating within modern law, and language arts.

Tools of expression potentially communicate both lies and truth. Mathematics have been used to skew statistics, but math has also been adapted by many godly scientists, like the ones listed on page 144, to discover scientific treasures needed to treat diseases, to build engines, to develop light bulbs and petroleum oil so that the extermination of whales for whale oil ceased, and whole communities stopped burning down due to faulty gas lighting systems.

Much of Christianity is dedicated to the acknowledgment of suffering and comforting those in persecution. While it is true that prejudice, suffering and death are genuine realities, the original image sustained in our world and in our existence should not be overshadowed or downplayed. God's creativity in nature is ongoing, and we exalt with His own reverie and redemption every day! Are the leaves still growing or turning colors? Are there still reflections of glory in the lakes, pools, and oceans in our world? Are animals still breeding and leaping and showing off their wonders and labors for your enjoyment? As artists, we should be detailing, and bragging on, and rejoicing in the liveliness and courage of nature, nature which continues to declare God's glory despite the terrible suffering it endures at the hands of humankind.

How would you feel if you created an entire fantasy world for viewers and characters, and those viewers and characters only declared their suffering at their own hands? What if all they could preach about were warnings, limits of grace, or the terror and persecutions to come? What if the enlightenment of today's marvels the hope, the joy and glory, were never encouraged, praised, or enjoyed? Wouldn't you be miffed?

I say, paint and write with God's authority. Pomegranates in the temple! Votes? I say we delve into our treasures in nature and herald our common, not-so-common, blessings through creativity filled with finesse. *Welcome to this creative party!* This, too, is a profound expression of holy creativity.

Consider whether to use the value of magic versus miracle as semiotic of spiritual mysteries. Since these devices utilize unnatural powers to transcend reality's limits, when using this technique, be careful not to be deceived yourself. To use it for Biblical images, do your research and ask the Holy Spirit to give insight and stop you as needed. Moses used God's power to bring water splashing from a rock for thirsty followers.[21] Was it magic or mystic? My father and I were especially moved by the way Allen Arnold used the technique of mystery and magic in his allegorical book, *The Story of With,* to expound on the purpose of loss, fear, love, and victory as used in the hand of the Holy or by the hand of evil.[22]

Charmayne Hafen, a talented author, uses magic in her book, "INDEBTED: The Berkshire Dragon," to exploit the allure of greed and the trickery of evil. Fear, loathing, death, and destruction are brought into perspective and detail. She contrasts the dragon's destructive powers with the transformative power and loyalty of friendship found in a neighboring kingdom.[23]

Perverse answers of all kinds are offered in books and media because imagination is quickened with trickery and the message will sell. Magic tickles the senses, mimicking wonder, power. But whose power is it? All fraud is deceitful and wicked. Meanwhile, children of God have direct access to the mysteries of this Wonderful Counselor as we are trained by Him and enjoy personal guidance through the Holy Spirit. Though we may have to wait for His emphasis to be revealed, we can work.

Honest enlightenment acts like yeast worked into a ball of dough. Luke recorded this mysterious action when Jesus said, "To what shall I compare the kingdom of God? It is like leaven that a woman took and hid in three measures of flour, until it was all leavened."[24] The Holy Spirit is readily available to those who cry out to God for help.[25] Seek wisdom earnestly in His ancient paths for semiotic clues to transcending evil.

Proverbs 9:9–11 says, "Give instruction to a wise man and he will be still wiser, Teach a righteous man and he will increase his learning. *The fear of the LORD is the beginning of wisdom, And the knowledge of the Holy One is understanding.* For by me your days will be multiplied, And years of life will be added to you...." (NASB).

What a reward is indicated, is *promised!* Our future glorification is God's promised reward for the righteous; the "glory" of which Paul writes in Romans 2:7–10 and 5:2. This is because our future glorification is hinged on God's own glory, which He gives portions of as teasers to us every day.

Bob Deffinbaugh points out in his message on Romans 8, that in the beginning, "Israel's glory was her God (1 Samuel 15:29). Glory belonged only to Him (1 Chronicles 29:11). Israel's response to God's glory was to glorify Him in worship (1 Chronicles 16:29). Even sinners were to give glory to God (*See*, Joshua 7:19; 1 Samuel 6:5). Israel was not to worship idols because this would give glory to mere images, rather than to God. But beyond glorifying God in worship, Israel was to tell the nations of God's glory (1 Chronicles 16:24). This is the heart of evangelism, then and now."[26] In whatever depiction, creatives are called to reach out to others with what they understand of God's glory in every situation.

Mysteries and espionage genres, thrillers, use science fiction or new discoveries in science to build their plots in the establishment of modern intelligence agencies with highly volatile political issues, which are reflections of human temptations magnified on a national scale or in global settings. Don't be afraid to use cutting edge discoveries and theories of science set against the mental psychosis or needs of the human heart. Use high finance, or gang-banging cultures together with history or futurism. Exploit the symbols of our humanity in your craft. Use the symbols of heroic sacrifices and victories as well. In all creation, God intended for the invocation and our intake systems to inform us about His love for us, intuitively, and His right to us. These things inform us, through right-brain ingenuity, of what we are unable to know by any other form of God's expression. Your artistic voice comes from revelation from God's Word as applied to the situation. Read it. Listen to it.

Think about it. God created all the brain cortexes (gray matter), and the connective tissue (white matter) that allows the cortexes to communicate together.

Do our authors, preachers, counselors, and teachers ever promote mistaken ideas or quotes? Of course, they do. Let's acknowledge that each one in the body has a purpose, and each one seeks to perform that purpose. Yet, there are holes in each of us, personal limits, and that is why we need to bear with each other. That is why we need every creative compassion of God.

I am not a numbers person, but when I began an arts management business, science and numbers held me to a certain standard of fact and truth. Fudging numbers does not change the truth. The numbers themselves challenged and motivated me. They caused me to wrestle with the LORD's purposes in my world. Creativity is the ability to step into things unseen, letting both science and the facts be true. Accept where you are. Trust God. Take note of the road signs. Practice the science of faith.

Your symbols and signs have their own story to tell. The LORD didn't make a mistake when he set you down in time, in place, with your boundaries and experiences. When life hands you lemons, you may be able to make lemonade, but there will be times when the appropriate response is to throw them against the wall and feel the acrid burn. We have learned that our senses are fundamentally good. Yes, art grips your sensual interest.

Then, there are times we are prohibited from seeing something of glory for an unknown reason. One evening, as I was turning out of a street in a valley, I noticed the bright streaks in the sky overhead. I pulled my car over to get out and take a better look at the sky. Someone passing me almost hit me standing in the street and laid on the horn. I returned to my car and raced to get out of the valley and onto the hill so that I could fully enjoy the display of the setting sun. But, the stoplight kept me waiting in limbo for an extraordinary length of time. By the time I finally found a knoll, there were high rises and cranes impeding my view. Just then, my irritation at God spilled over into angry words: "Why did You prevent me from enjoying such an incredible view?" I demanded. Embarrassed, I began to laugh at my thoughts of entitlement. Obviously, He could have rearranged the moments and the geography for my pleasure, but He didn't. I felt dejected with my misfortune. The loss now serves a point. Not all art is created for all eyes and ears.

A good writer will indulge the imagination to utilize all techniques available to make life vibrate.

Christian creatives can be life-giving in the analysis of national media, city arts events, or local political dilemmas. Ask for His wisdom, and tread carefully. Remember that politicians and agencies have agendas. Sometimes those agendas are hidden in a proposed action and statistics and testimonies are engineered.

SHORT LIST OF SCIENTISTS WHO
BELIEVED SCRIPTURE

Scientist	Discovery	Faith
Galileo Galilei	the New Science	Catholic
Antoine Laurent Lavoisier	the Revolution in Chemistry	Catholic
Johannes Kepler	Motion of the Planets	Lutheran
Nicolaus Copernicus	the Heliocentric Universe	Catholic (priest)
Michael Faraday	the Classical Field Theory	Sandemanian
James Clerk Maxwell	Electromagnetic Fields	Presbyterian; Anglican; Baptist
Enrico Fermi	Atomic Physics	Catholic
Leonard Euler	Eighteenth-Century Math	Calvinist
Max Born	Quantum Mechanics	Jewish Lutheran
Franz Boas	Modern Anthropology	Jewish
Werner Heisenberg	Quantum Theory	Lutheran
Claude Levi-Strauss	Structural Anthropology	Jewish
Lynn Margulis	Symbiosis Theory	Jewish
Karl Landsteiner	the Blood Groups	Jewish
Louis Pasteur	the Germ Theory of Disease	Catholic
Carl Linnaeus	the Binomial Nomenclature	Christianity

| Anton van Leeuwenhoek | the Simple Microscope | Dutch Reformed |

LAYERS OF LEARNING IN LOGOS

It wasn't that the work of God, in the wonder of the eclipse, was underwhelming to me, which I pronounced as "bleh" to others.

No, when I considered the fact that I was, yes, underwhelmed – as I often am – with the sky, with nature, agitated with the heat of summer, sighing at the height of the grass to mow, put out with the danger of blizzards and hurricanes – I realized that I have a spirit of arrogance, entitlement!

God has secret treasures and systems in science, delicate purposes that He likes to keep to Himself. "Yes, I'm holding card," He flaunts. "It's up to you to watch the game closely enough to figure out the hand I am holding. What is my strategy? Why should I let you in on it?"

When I was walking around the lake this morning, the thought suddenly came to me: Girl, you get your best pictures around this lake. The sunrises and sunsets cast in this pond have delighted you in your Maker. Why then, didn't you plan to come here to capture the eclipse that just occurred? The very next thought was that I have spent zippo time, nada, learning the significance of heavenly bodies related to everything else in life. I have no context to appreciate the math, or science, or hue of photography, of timing of what just happened. I've been a lazy student of the Great Party of Life. It isn't God's work that is underwhelming. It is mine.

Reading about the character of God is not the same thing as seeing His beautiful gifts in nature on the big screen. Neither experience is as good as walking with Him in the sunset by a lake and relaying your delight to Him for the twitters, warbles, chip-chips, the wingspans soaring overhead, and ducks landing on webbed skis in wakes disturbing the reflective surface water, or the humor of coming too close to baby goslings protected by hissing geese. Reading about God's grace or mercy is not the same as experiencing a rescue from harm or from self-destruction, but writing about it can solidify trust and important values.

Droll-humor can discount a joy spawned by hyperbole and used properly to make a point. Figures of speech woo spiritual imagination, too. Scripture is full of figures of speech!

Hyperbole is not the same as lying. Who said it? "Seven hundred select troops were left-handed, each of whom could sling a stone at a hair and not miss,"[27] or, *"The rock poured me out rivers of oil,"* [28] or, "Him that overcomes will I make a pillar in the temple of my God, and he shall go out no more,"[29] or, *"The cities are great, and walled up to heaven."*[80] How about this metaphor: "I ate your words, and they were sweet to my taste." The wise use of figures of speech is a tool authorized to sweeten the journey to understanding.

On the road to Emmaus, the disciples of Jesus walked and talked with someone whom they believed to be a stranger. They were able to inquire about the Word as it applied to their lives, and the stranger answered.

Then the LORD opened their eyes and revealed to them His identity.[31] Had their physical eyelids been closed? No, this is creative hyperbole. As Amy Pierson from Burning Heart Workshops points out, "In their recognition of the experience, the person and the Word, a white matter link was made between the brain's cortexes. This journey is both literal and spiritual."[32] They at first do not recognize Jesus, maybe God is purposely blinding their eyes. They begin to understand what the Scripture says about Him. Then, they recognize Him for who He is, and finally they give witness of what they have experienced of Him with their own voice. The pieces fell together from a variety of forms of communication and in such a profound personal journey, that the men became courageous and even willing martyrs for their truth.

Don't misjudge the value of science fiction, modern films, fantasy, and poetry (antiquated or modern), often read in pubs, against the standards held for a child's education.

Literature meant for adults may include sensuality in the course of a meaningful story. It may depict a person's steps to various dead ends and out as they seek the truth or redemption. Sometimes adult literature is treated as wicked. It is nervously censored prior to the author's purpose of this communication even being absorbed.

RELAX. If you have heard good reviews about a book, try it out. Learn from it. Limiting an adult's ability to learn by what's appropriate for a child and calling that "Christian" is to misrepresent the vast imagination God

170

intended for us to use. Adults need and can also understand some of the bunny trails others take to find truth, love, and redemption, because honestly, we have taken some of those trails ourselves. Depicting them, seeing them, may erupt in new understanding, or courage to admit the truth, gaining some much-needed humility or counsel. Symbols of another's experience may breed honesty or humility to gain counsel sharing with someone else. These steps may help to form a unified vision or a few steps into redemption.

A dinky example of this is when I announced on social media, "Pretty ticked off at the hordes of copulating Japanese beetles in our vines and rose beds! In two days, they've left thousands of innocent leaves pocked with holes creating a web of what's left! I put out two bags of insecticide to catch them, and though they are filling up with beetles, the sounds of the cha-cha flowing from the vine made me look a little closer. They were there, shining beautifully fluorescent, wings fluttering in little undulating pyramids atop so many beds of leaves. I wonder who will win?" Within a moment, someone offered advice: "Get frogs."

The whole Earth is filled with God's glory declares Isaiah 6:3, but did the Creator design the universe with hashtags and points nailed into the bark of every living tree to make sure we didn't miss it? Did He write calligraphy verses under every sunset, rushing river, or dying bug to make sure that we completely understood each image? This is one way in which He is deemed holy, uniquely above everyone else, exclaimed Isaiah, and perhaps Isaiah's shout #HolyHolyHoly!

In fact, Psalm 19 says, The heavens declare God's handiwork *apart from words.* The heavens and firmament have no language. But, day after day and night after night, they are signing *words* about the attributes of their Creator through moving symbols to all the living. A lot of mystery hounds us throughout life, doesn't it? God wants us to play in these symbolic wonders throughout every phase of life and to recognize these signs of seasons, and of light and dark as He opens our eyes. He wants us to seek Him and praise Him with and without words.

I have cried sitting at the table of a talented cook. The art of the presentation and tastes made me want to try harder, but also made me weak with the understanding that I do not possess such talents. I am only the recipient of grace. When I experienced these truths, returning thanks with tears to the chef, I understood the difference between pragmatic meal preparation and the frivolous pleasure of an artist's detail in the kitchen. Nurture with hospitality.

Suppose, alternatively, that we are seeking our own fame, working night and day to display ripped muscles never to be used for God's glory. Or suppose we are seeking our own pride by touting religious sounding opinions, or by flouting publicly that we've grasped the edges of the universe. We may want to repurpose many things for ourselves to possess or control others. We may seek these things, uninterrupted, with particularly crafted nuance. Surging along in our pride, we stumble upon a symbolic surprise in a book, or a movie, in a wedding ceremony, or at the opera. Maybe a foreign flick causes the truth to surface in parallel journeys or cultural images. Isn't it good for our souls to be stirred and investigated, touched by other stories?

When symbols reach us, humble us, we recognize our own need. We can become recipients of these gifts. Stories can move us along to gratitude, to courage, to humility, to love, and to justice.

God uses many forms of art to remind us that there are reasons for fantastical things, beyond words. We are recipients of grace. Dizzy Gillespie, the musician who wrote *A Night in Tunisia* (a.k.a. Interlude), expressed exotic delight by orchestrating a complex bass line in the "A section," which avoided the standard jazz walking bass pattern and, also by using oscillating half-step-up V chord changes with half-step-down Sub V chords.[33] These elements give the song a unique, mysterious flavor.

Later, Ella Fitzgerald was moved to write the lyrics for this desert fantasy enjoyed in popular jazz clubs. Riding a camel over trails in a Tunisian desert may have been too wonderful to comprehend even if God-sized hashtags in our mother tongue were plastered on banners overhead. So, He gave us jazz.

Sometimes, Christians prefer rules and manageable memes and doctrines. But, recently, I realized that Jesus Himself went out without knowing where He was going. Yup. "He went out, not knowing where He was going" (Hebrews 11:8). There comes a time when we must let go and walk in faith. We must choose the flow of consciousness and trust our creative minds, trust God. Let go of the handle bars and just let ourselves create the story—almost watching as it evolves from somewhere unknown, somewhere in our subconscious.

Publishers of today seek authors, film writers, scoring musicians, fine actors, and set designers who can wield such a degree of excellence that disbelief is suspended and life's mysteries are unraveled in dramatic symbols (A-ha! moments). Even advertisements are successful when an A-ha! moment can be crafted into a sales pitch. These bright treasures are made available to an artist's hand through Scripture's own semiotic tales. They are within the reach of the creative arm when a soul is thirsty. In the image of Luke 13:7–9, the owner of a dead fig tree begs for another year of patience and more fertilizer as a beautiful reminder of Christ's desire to save dying souls. Come, seek out the Biblical Christ, the magnificent Creator, and find Him to be the fresh expression pouring into your art.

God used a writer's prophetic image to benefit a heathen king as the protagonist in a story found in Isaiah 45:2–5. When God's people showed the ruler that God had called him by name, Cyrus, and anointed Him, Cyrus heard the LORD's promise:

> I will go before you and make the rough places smooth; I will shatter the doors of bronze and cut through their iron bars. *I will give you the treasures of darkness And hidden wealth of secret places, So that you may know that it is I, The LORD, the God of Israel, who calls you by your name.* I am the LORD,

and there is no other; Besides Me, there is no God. I will gird you, though you have not known Me.

And when the Hebrews showed Cyrus, in their sacred scroll, what had been prophesied of him by name 150 years earlier, Cyrus obeyed the calling of the Hebrew God to free the Hebrews from slavery and exile, bringing them back to their homeland.[34] The Almighty's breadcrumb trail had only to feed the *stampcrab* wonder, and Cyrus turned into an uncanny freedom angel. *These tribal names, facts, and truths still matter to a Biblical worldview.*

God uses this experience of Cyrus and of the Hebrews coming out of exile as a continuing example and promise of His Word that anyone might also grasp onto the knotted threads of it for the sake of Jacob, God's servant, and Israel, God's chosen one. What is the key for the creative? It's to know the LORD Jehovah, that there is no other God to trust. We can trust Him to equip us properly, to strengthen and protect us, even to remove the power to what kings have set in place.

As I was writing an essay on writing, I saw a stunning quote from a Jewess, a German woman, who has resonated her intelligence and influence into many vessels in this world. I suppose it was all the more stunning to me because it appeared as the precise issue I was grappling with in writing this book. "Storytelling reveals meaning without committing the error of defining it."—Hannah Arendt.[35]

I will read more about her conflicted life and relished work, I already have done so, simply because of this quote. Forgive me the error of using definitions to describe the elephant in the Kingdom.

Can God use non-Christians as the hero or heroine in a book written by a Christian with a Christian worldview? Just look at Cyrus. Look at Pontius Pilot and how God used and redeemed His actions to grant salvation to the world.[36] All men and women are servants of God, in fact. All kings of the earth will bring Him tribute.[37] Everything that has breath will praise Him.[38] Even if we choose not to serve the LORD, but to serve the devil, yet the One Who is sovereign over all will still work through every sleight of hand to bring about His good will and to offer His love and redemption for whomever sincerely responds. Will you as a creative, personally, be treated better than a servant? Will the Almighty recognize you as His beloved?

Rule 7: REVEAL. Find parallels and layers to unfold. Test to reveal whether any symbolic word is from God. Does it complement or conflict with what God has already revealed?

8.

NURTURE CREATIVES

"By seeking and blundering we learn." This quote is attributed to Johann Wolfgang Goethe, the greatest German literary figure alive between 1700-1900, also a playwright, a diplomat, and an anthropologist.

I found "seeking and blundering" painted on the elevator wall backstage in the Denver Performing Arts Center and photographed it to remember I am not alone. By this, I was also reminded of the patient experimentation and failure along the road to success by the head of a famous marketing company who confessed he was mortified repeatedly by his many failures; failures in marketing, fortunately, are failures exactly because people don't pay attention. It was his successes that astounded people and provided the finance upon which he built his storytelling career.

Not only do we need to be patient with ourselves as we experiment and refine, but we also need to be patient and nurturing with others in their craft.

When I mentioned to a cover designer that this book included a section on nurturing creatives, Tracy laughed. "Isn't that like herding cats?"

Obviously, there are many sources of nurturing.

Nurturing is readily — and scientifically — acknowledged as starting in the womb.

After fertilization, at the beginning of every human life is the embryo stage where biology of the multicellular physics develops into organs, and bodily structures. We don't often connect the dots between this stage and the embryo's need for air, but let's do that.

An embryo is connected to his or her mother for nourishment through an umbilical cord that is only cut and tied off at birth. An embryo is completely dependent upon the mother for blood and safety to survive through fetal stages.

Blood is created for the mother and child by the oxygen which is taken in through the mother.

We say a mother nurtures her child in the womb with air intake, water and food. She also denies herself certain pleasures and privileges in order to maintain the welfare of her unborn child. But, when the umbilical cord is cut, does the baby become completely independent? No.

The baby's body instinctively learns to breathe through his or her mouth, nose and the pumping of independent lungs. A baby learns to suck nourishment, and these are the first signs of a body's craving to live, and to get life by instinct. Dependence and inner dependence, then emancipation, is the cycle of living that allows for creative accomplishment in any field or endeavor.

Yet, in stage after stage of growth, a child is

emancipated repeatedly from one type of dependance, one source of nurture, to another as each transition is achieved by instinct or by creativity.

At no time is a child's automated intake of air ever disconnected until death. The adult never becomes emancipated from air until death. To strangle a life or to deprive it of water or food is cruel and assumed to be the opposite of nurture.

Forms of nurture include the following.

a) Spiritual teaching and guidance. When a child is taught spiritual counsel, core aspects of hope, safety, morality, and decision making are provided on which to build psychological health. When spiritual nurture is abdicated and any form of immoral assault surrounds a child, the psyche becomes wounded and stunted, even perverted or ill.

b) Teaching the ability to forage for food, to hunt, kill, gather, cook and bake provide another source of knowledge, wisdom, and wonder for nature.

c) Training physical prowess is nurtured through bodily and mental exercise, learning tactical rules.

d) Tutoring language arts, reading, mathematics, and science in a child so that a mind can do more than survive into adulthood. A nurtured life can thrive into specified technical areas of honed skill. Houses are engineered and built with communication skills, engineering, learned soil and topography, and how to mathematically figure the structural loads that can be born upon walls. How does a chimney work on the cold side of the house compared to the warm side?

How does the staircase support the structure? How does the rise of the roof beautify the façade? How should the flow of the residential streets be designed to and from parks, lakes, shopping areas, and industrial services? A specialized form of training and nurture is required to learn to apply such knowledge in wisdom.

e) The biological, chemical make up of plants, algae, earth, mammals, and marsupials make up the sciences of perfume and medical treatment.

These careers are specially nurtured.

So, we understand then, that casting a vision, leading an exploration, finding adventure and letting curiosity play out to hypothetical ends is a huge part of how someone is nurtured. Correction, admonition, and refocusing one's attention on a honed skill generates expertise, a journeyman's license, a graduation, and further successes.

Nurture often calls for the supply of finance to succeed. Grants, loans, personal philanthropy, gifts appropriate for rites of passage are forms of nurture.

RETURN A JUST REWARD TO WHOM IT IS DUE

I recently heard a jazz musician playing his horn beautifully in Central Park. He was fairly old. I gave him two bucks and took a video on my phone. I will never forgive myself. It haunts me wondering whether he can afford insurance. Do I think that God can't provide for my needs if I give freely to street artists?

Is His arm too short? This dilemma for me, this problem with underwriting a creative project or acknowledging the maker-giver, nurturing a talent, and returning thanks for a creative offering runs not only vertically to God, but also horizontally to artists.

Encountering that musician at that time caused me to reexamine my benevolence, or lack thereof, and my giving priorities. What happened there? Did one creative snub another by giving a customary tip for menial service? Do I relegate other artists to beggars' wages by assuming they earn their living by other means? Do I suffer from a ignorance or bias regarding the poverty of other creatives in substandard living conditions?

Why do *you* think there are so many homeless creatives and street artists? Mimes under a bridge? Who pays their grocery bill, their education bill, or their medical bills? Although industrious creatives have a plan, the marketing channels may abruptly change. Maybe the craft of an artist rollercoasters due to shut downs of a venue, market demand, or it goes out of fashion after a few years. Proverbs 3:27–29 tells us, "Do not withhold good from whom it is due." If it is within the reach of your hand, pay a person for his or her work today, in the moment, not with a promise of things to come tomorrow. Even if you are not the primary beneficiary of the work, it is better to reach out your hand with a just reward and with grace when a person has worked honestly for something but has not yet been paid.

- When creatives do something truly amazing, they want their family to see what came out of them and to be as amazed as they are about it. Sometimes they want to claim all the credit even though they had no idea they could pull it off. (There must be a God, right?)
- When creatives play music to create love between two people, memorializing landmarks in life, they understand the value of their gifts and skills.
- When a creative waits for her friend to stop with the office gossip in order to call her friend's attention to listen to a poem she wrote, she is really yearning for her friend to meditate a few holy moments on something that matters more. *It takes just a minute to listen to get it.*
- If someone with the means to help a creative publish a first storybook approaches, the offer wouldn't be turned down. (And, a friend's help finding teachers to buy this story for students would not receive an upturned nose, either!) *Do you know this person?*
- Creatives can't stop creating because they love the wonder of the process and a new result.

Too often good songwriters and spiritual singers fail to get paid. They often can't bill for ministry services unless a company hires them. They appear to beg for tips by setting out a jar or a hat. They sometimes get applause, and they sometimes get compliments or write-ups, but they often don't get the assurance of a roof over their heads at night from their hard work, education, and time spent to develop something pleasing or gripping to the soul.

In days past, many artists and composers had patrons who nurtured, promoted, and supported them. Now, often, choices for Christian artists are relegated to late night bars and summer jobs drawing portraits at amusement parks.

> "Try creating a replica of a Cezanne or a Matisse and you'll see how humbling it is." – Tess Callahan

Why do we take beauty and delight for granted? Why, when it is within our power to honor or bless a hard worker, do we resist giving what is appropriate to him or her as rightful earnings? We can even fail to return thanks to the Giver for these creative gifts.

People with business acumen and other good people are often ignorant of the value and need for the Christian worldview to find sway in media. Do you resort to judgment or critique of our mainstream media, books, and music but fail to stimulate change in your critique by offering hope or good news?

Christian imagination needs to be nurtured and supported in a big way, a much bigger way for your good, for my good, and for the greater glory of God.

Christians who have the financial means need to invest in creatives they trust, and not allow them to worry about where their next meal is coming from, or how to put gas in their tanks.

I'm not going to harp on the dilemma that most Christian creatives experience trying to put a roof over their head and food in their mouths through their artistry and work. This cross relates to the cross of our creative forerunner, Christ. Our present suffering is preparatory and a prerequisite to future glorification.[1] The Creator may miraculously transform your trials of poverty into blessings, but perhaps the real miracle is when members of Christ's Church transform the poverty of their maker community into success and health.

What I do hope the raft of leaders and less creative people consider is that children learn respect, gratitude, and whether a payment is honest or dishonest from their parents' attitudes. Artists create because God the Father is the Creator. They will create even if they starve. As an outsider, you may believe artists are being belligerent against social norms. Why then, if the price of creating is perhaps freezing to death, would they choose those odds? It is because creating is at the core, the hub, of what God put inside of them to do. They get carried away...

Annie Sullivan proved, through her individual focus on the life of Helen Keller, that carrying the Word to others is much more than the written word. It includes a compassionate reach. It includes the personal touch of a mentor. It requires kindness, foresight, persistent nurturing, correction, and vision as well as tutelage.[2]

Capture Books publishes interactive consumable

books like Diane Andrews' *MY STEP JOURNAL: 365 Days Into Intimacy with God*.[3] This journal doesn't tell you to pray a set prayer. Instead, it helps you remember situations and piece together episodes of your personal life to make sense of your story and to write your legacy. In 365 DAYS INTO INTIMACY WITH GOD, you write down an answer to one question per day with one Scripture for a writing prompt.

SOOTHING RAIN is a conversational study that leaps off the pages of the workbook into women's groups. Casual friends can grow together as they listen to each other's experiences and perspectives. *SOOTHING RAIN* is a delightful mentoring tool, which provokes discussion about diverse answers to the proposed situations. When people converse about Biblical responses to their situations, we grow in empathy and in knowledge.[4]

Nurturing often requires food, a bed, and transportation as well as a word aptly placed. Annie Sullivan was willing to be the hands of God, the potter, forming and wrestling with raw, unwieldable clay. She lost the tip of her little pinky to form that clay on the potter's wheel. Helen Keller bit it off.[5] Was her expression fully alive and creative? Didn't it highlight the God who transforms a caged soul, trapped in the collapse of bodily systems, into becoming a great recipient of His glory?

In college, my mentor and music professor introduced his classroom to the booklet by Francis

Schaeffer, *ART AND THE BIBLE*. In it, he declared,

"The Lordship of Christ should include an interest in the arts. A Christian should use these arts to the glory of God, not just as tracts, mind you, but as things of beauty to the praise of God."[6]

Someone out there named Francis was in the business of encouraging musicians, artists, writers, and filmmakers to create all kinds of experiential art. Not just Scripture art. Not just evangelical messages. His reasoning was circular. He presented many Biblical records of God's designs for the temple, for the priests' clothing, for the arc in the tabernacle, for the priestly music from Moses, Miriam, David, the Sons of Korah, and Asaph. The furniture was designed together with pillars and interior décor. Schaeffer also detailed King Solomon's civic glories including architecture and music *outside of religious ritual or sentiment.*[7]

This little booklet planted in me the seed that God loves frivolous creations! He is pleased when we wield any form of art for any purpose that does not rebel against His goodness. There seems to be no pragmatic reason for dictating the colors of the décor, or the shapes or the materials. It seems God was being frivolous and dictating frivolous beauty, why? Because He could. Because He can. And, when we mimic Him, we can enjoy this same frivolous extravagance!

Have you spoken harshly to your son or daughter, employee, mother, father, or friend for wasting time daydreaming? What if the daydreamer was actually contemplating how to word an important letter, or what if they were trying to figure out the meaning to something they had just witnessed, or what if they were trying to memorize a turn of phrase because it seemed important enough to remember? What if reverie is the first sprout of a germinating seed in creative expression? What if they were, in wonder, praising God for the beautiful outdoors?

You nurture your soul when you allow yourself to spend quality time daydreaming or enjoying breathtaking expressions of creativity.

When you've been reading, writing, doodling, watching a great show, or working on a poem, don't betray the value of God's beating heart for the whims of artistry inside you. Mention and exclaim openly His work to others. Open eyes to the wonder, and let conversations roll for His purposes.

These are the extravagant times when your ideas are forming, and your practice is being honed, and when you are delighting in mimicking your Creator's own sensationalism.

The Lord not only offers a doorway to a blessed place of belonging for each artist, singer, songwriter, and poet—the Lord is offering to come through the door and reside inside of the creative, to bring life to the seeds and raw elements maker types. We belong in Him. He belongs in us. If this is true, then let's determine to be trend-setters for launching godly creatives, shall we? Capture Books aims to encourage real creative experiences and community through books, book clubs, crafting, engineering and manufacturing, writing clubs, and by conversational inclusive Bible studies. Are you involved in a writer's critique group? A singing or drama focused group? An engineering group? A support group? A helping group? Christians ought to be leaders in the maker culture.

BEING RIGHTEOUS IN BAD SITUATIONS

Righteousness is a Biblical mindset to find a creative path to life. It seeks to nurture every ounce of good from a BAD situation. This is the difference between being righteous in wisdom and just being moral or ethical. Righteousness breeds regeneration through a relationship with the Living God. Morality alone can end in lifelessness or condemnation. Ethics can end in empty wins, or in judgment and punishment. There are two camps on the misuse of guns and mass killings out there. One focuses on the gun laws, the other focuses on mental health systems. Many on both sides believe that taking God and Creationism out of the schools has left children without a hub or core of hope.

Shutting down the play and cursing the system or the actors when something terrible is being depicted, or when something is being depicted *terribly*, is a short sale. Be righteous by depicting a good and active Creator and ways to walk with God.

In our historical novel, *THE WHISPERING OF*

THE WILLOWS, set in Appalachia, the author, Tonya Jewel Blessing, includes two quick but haunting landmarks in the life of fourteen-year-old Emerald Ashby, events that change the trajectory of her future. The reader cannot squirm out of them. This is a true picture of life.[8]

Everyone suffers from something. We each learn to make peace with what ails us through faith, through creativity, and through wise applications of what we're handed as life tools to work ourselves out of a crucible. Instead of preventing a teen from reading about the dysfunction of poverty and a rape experience, parents who believe in the redemptive purposes of a good God might take the time to winnow thoughts of reality, hope, and purpose to kids exposed to those scenes. Kids are not as naïve as we believe. Perhaps trapping students who are going through puberty into a corner of naiveté prevents them from growing into their own solid faith, into a deeper knowledge of God.

A parent or counselor may need to read the book together with the teen or form a mother-daughter book club to discuss the differences that actually do exist between genders. Measured exposure to social truths provides an opportunity to discuss a variety of ways in which Christians can help to rescue teen girls from a downward spiral after a rape occurs. This is a worthy aim. This is exactly the kind of creative opportunity that arises from our book, *The WHISPERING OF THE WILLOWS.*

In a world where kids are being told there is no real gender to consider, Tonya Jewel Blessing shows the explicit differences that affect young women experiencing a rape or any premature sexual activity. It also provides real hope and the miracle of transformation within a loving community. Someone who steps in to parent an at-risk teen is honored in the Willows. God's provision is highlighted through heroic people, heroic choices, lyrics of old Appalachian hymns, and exposing the nonsense of superstitious beliefs.[9]

G.K. Johnson's novel, *THE ZEALOTS*, walks readers through the pressures of injustice and the choices presented by two different communities of faith during the first century in Roman occupied Judea. This story appeals to the hearts and minds of young men who can easily resort to violence and retribution and presents there, a higher calling.

In the child's story, PRINCESS LILLIAN AND GRANDPA'S GOODBYE, Jenny Fulton and Indra Grace Hunter portray the importance of two world's coexisting, and how Christian parents can mentor a child not only in Native American Indian traditions, but also in Christian truths.

One's belief system can be anchored and trained by one's community.

Art is often intended to be experienced in the community and for the good purpose of discussion and group engagement. In the beginning, God communicated *among* the three persons of the One

Godhead to create a *place of belonging for a community, His*. All of nature became home for a community. Separating the sea from the land, the Creator put the earth into a *safe* rotation in which animals, vegetation, and human beings *could survive and flourish*. The apostle Paul instructs leaders in the church to equip others, disciple, and lift up their gifts.[10] We are to be inclusive in our stories of community.

The Almighty empowered musical creatives with scored notes on a page and played-by-ear music to speak to the right-brain of every individual without the use of words (vibrating force, instrument tone, and personal technique). *Music felled the walls of Jericho!*[11]

When we consider the mystery and power of the gift of music for goodness' sake, and we know of those who wield the power to play it skillfully, we advocate for them using the proper platform for what God Himself has endowed to them. Why not enjoy playing host or act as a marketing agent and invite friends to a house concert. Tell your boss about their talent with a note for the next office party. Offer an accounting service or business advice for their first year of budgeting. Trade services. Pay a bill, lend a car, give them a guestroom in your house to help them get established. Be a mentor. Lend them your copy of *Being Creative!*

Christians working as editors, producers, and actors in Hollywood understand that holding back evil is a wise and difficult aspect of their occupations. Heated debates, exasperated timelines, and personalities often pull rank, but God is using His own creatives in the industry to offer substitute scenes and different renderings of diabolical scenes.

C.E.O.'s and builders of worship centers often employ artists because creatives can create that special factor to bring in the people and make them feel something, make them stay.

The Creator ordained that the voice of the LORD is far from complete without artistry. The voice of the LORD is far from dynamic without artistry. If the LORD uses the priorities of creativity and relationship, then He knows what is best to convey the LOGOS.

Attorneys arguing to persuade judges and juries utilize drama, creativity, word craft, strategy, science, statistics, and logic.

Powerful people understand the value of artists' work, and they are instructed in Scripture not to exploit or use these people for gain (without paying them what is due).[12]

Why does theft of art and exploitation of creatives continue to occur in our world, in our places of worship, and in our sites of learning? Does the audience believe that talent is not the same thing as work, that an artist should share his or her gifts freely?

Those who usually employ the left-brain curriculum for creativity include technicians, editors, and teachers. Words are used in expressive senses to paint word-pictures, to persuade, to clarify vagaries, and to instruct in knowledge and technique. They may take issue with artistic messages that are not spelled out for them. Yet, God intended for left- and right-brained people to work together, to honor each other, and learn to keep communicating.

God wants us to mimic Him in community and relationships through expressive and taciturn art forms. He means for us to understand each other better and to experience Him more.

THE HAPPY LINGUISTICS OF GOD

The meaning of language has morphed into the age of technology. Artists may work in Adobe, InDesign or in Word Docx, yet not understand each other's coding or how to translate from a PDF to HTML, from an ebook for Kindle to an ePub for Apple. There are political prejudices and competition in social media platforms which prevents some messages from being broadcast to the recipients you aim to reach. Algorithms may be squashed, and not in your favor.

Conversion processes from one code or language to another code or language can be time-consuming and defeating to a big picture person since one language does not translate well to another. Different techies cannot speak each other's language. They can merely see and commend or critique another's end result. Is it well done? Is it an enviable piece? Is the work favored by the judges? Historically, video formats and televisions also used entirely different codes among emergent nations.

Knowing this makes it easier to accept that people perceive and understand communication sources differently. Some say, "all that matters is that love is communicated. God is love." But is love God? The devil is in the details and semantics can be twisted.

Language, spoken or unspoken, is the road to meaningful communication in any era, at any age. So, what happens when the meaning of codes and words get absorbed from one language into another? How important is it that some connotations and implications are distorted or lost?

A friend of mine is a linguist who translates scripture and Jesus films into a language for a middle eastern nation. But the implications of formal speech, poetic chanting for the Psalms, and casual youthful accents from the north to the central geography to the south hold differences which create opportunities for long debates in the process of translations. Some words understood well in their language mean very little to American or English readers. Much of the interpretation of each word, each phrase, is cultural. Language and semantics do matter.

Is there a language unique to God's people that is worthy of value for use in every culture?

ATTITUDES FORM LANGUAGE

The Italians have a word for trying to reclaim an

unworkable relationship, "cavoli riscaldati" or, reheated cabbage. Isn't it fitting? With a good look at various cultures, it becomes clear that there are a variety of addicting attitudes, and cultural bias, i.e., habits aligned with each one. Even Christians can and do get addicted to unhealthy ways of censoring messages, poor reasoning, unhealthy interpretations, mimicking circular philosophies, engaging in poor or cryptic means of communication.

The drug habit often stems from simply living in a culture of drugs. In a group recovery meeting I attended, one man complained about the daily pain he felt in his normal relationships and work experiences. He felt the road to recovery had only added new pain. "Everything feels too much of a drag, too personally expensive. What I need," he said, "is a miracle! I don't believe I can do this."

Someone responded, "We are all looking for miracles, some magic pill to solve our problems. But, stick with the program, get your sponsor and you'll see looking back that the miracle happened. It's the program. It's the work you do for yourself and for others even when you are in pain. It's God. It's the miracle of a community to go to; people who help you and tell you the truth. There's no magic pill. Magic pills got us into this mess."

Remember Leah, Jacob's first wife who was thrilled to name her maidservant's first son, "Gad"? The name means, "how fortunate!" Her exclamation meant, "I will be happy and envied!"[13] The experience of gaining an advantage over life's obstacles or disadvantages does bring on great feelings of happiness and an attitude of blessing.

My nephew is a collector of board games. He can speak a different language when introducing the various types of games to those willing to sit around the table and learn. Some games seem like pure luck or chance. Others take on a high degree of strategy. Some require comradery among players, others seem to create suspicion and anger toward the other players. Every game depends on the rules of a particular gaming language.

There are times when playing that I feel I have drawn the short stick. There's nothing left to do but play out my lot and be a good sport. Other times, I gain an advantage. Many times, I find myself praying about the game and searching my heart for what's important. Others in my circle laugh at that personal disclosure. "It's just a game," I've been told. But Scripture describes how God entered into the crazy game of Jacob's spotted and striped flocks when the deceitful Laban repeatedly tricked him. God caused the latent gene of spots and striped animals to flourish and gain advantage over Laban's trickery.[14] God multiplies ingenuity, investments, prosperity, and favor even outside of gravity and despite science.

There are times when people can only receive God's love language through an animal, usually a pet that they can hug and safely confide in. In the picture book, WILL YOU HOLD MY STORY? author Kathy

Joy invokes God's love language to a small child when no-one human has the time to stop and listen to the heavy story she carries. Isn't it profound and sweet that God turns away from verbal communication and the written word to fulfill His aim of communicating loving care through dumb nature?

When we talk about needing God's blessing, or we pray for God's blessing, on our marriage, on our travels, on our children, for our communities, in business affairs—we're asking for the Lord to circumvent our faults and the faults of others that may otherwise bring us to demise. We're invoking a heavenly intervention despite science. Blessings are not just words. Neither are blessings spells believers cast upon the water. These are prayers to invoke the power of God over our lives. Psalm 2:12 exclaims, "Kiss the Son, [...] Oh how blessed [happy, fortunate, and to be envied] are all those who seek refuge and put their trust in Him." Is that true?

How does God communicate with us?

Though Scripture describes people as being blessed, favored or fortunate–likely or unlikely–I often hear Christians today speak of amazing occurrences or blessings as though they were "magic," as in, "what a magical moment," or, "luck," as in, "I lucked out and found a wonderful woman," or, "as luck would have it..."

What is it about the idea of magic that seems better today to a Christian than being the recipient of everyday security and protection? Is it the isolation of our responsibility from the good result? Because, a gift given, whether a predictable result or not, requires the return of thanks to the one who grants the gift. Magical results have no such responsibility.

The usual return for good stewardship seems predictable. Yet, not everyone gets the same result for the same effort. Does God favor His people? Psalm 144:15 exclaims, "How [happy, blessed, enviable] are people in the case where the Lord is their God!" Is there special favor for those who live and walk with God in His community?

Synonyms of magic (n):	Illusion, sorcery, witchcraft, wizardry, necromancy, enchantment, alchemy, spell working, incantation, the supernatural, occultism, the occult, black magic, the black arts, devilry, divination, malediction, voodoo, hoodoo, sympathetic magic, white magic, witching, witchery
Synonyms of Magic (adj):	wonderful, exciting, hypnotic, fascinating, captivating, charming, glamorous, bewitching, magical, enchanting, entrancing, spellbinding, magnetic, irresistible

Wonder: (adj, n)	See Judges 13:17–20 for the name of The Angel of the Lord, is outside of human comprehension, secret
Luck (n):	chance considered as a force to make good or bad things happen for apparently no reason, Lady Luck, destiny, fortune, a twist of fate, lot in life, in the stars, karma, serendipity
Blessing (n):	protection, favor, grace, fortune, advantages. A blessing in disguise, undeserved mercy. Transformation.
Fortunate (adj):	wealthy in assets or possessions, blessing, happy, prosperous, healthy, protected, favored, graced, in a good position, safe-guarded, well situated, the recipient of a miracle or benefit
Fantasy (n):	imagination, creativity, fancy, invention, originality, vision, speculation, make-believe, daydreaming, reverie

Miracle (n):	In reality, a surprising and welcomed event that is not explained by science or natural occurrences. A highly improbable or unlikely event, extraordinary development, marvel, divine intervention, mystery, sign

There was a time when I prayed daily for vindication in unjust persecutions where a series of zoning laws, building codes, and lawsuits were launched against my husband and me because we had built a Christian hospitality house. Eventually, I came to understand that God's favor presides beyond and in spite of human trickery, poor judges, difficult rules and legalese. Juries who are not told the dates, the facts, or the truth may not realize an attorney's sleight of hand. Yet, God does vindicate His own! He is not beholden to powerful cities or governments, though they often win their objective initially.

Psalm 128:2 exclaims, "For you shall eat the fruit of the labor of your hands. Happy and enviable will you be, and it *shall be well with you.*"

Yahweh invented the idea of the phoenix. He's called it rising from the dead, finding redemption, being adopted, and being transferred from the kingdom of darkness into the kingdom of light. He invites us into deliverance, saving grace, miracles, generosity, kindness, wonders, God's favor, mercy, salvation, fortitude, irony, or endurance—an apt word like a golden apple set in a silver lining. It is seen that, "His mercies are new every morning. Great is Your faithfulness, oh, God!"[15]

There also seems to be an unusual return for those who listen to wisdom and learn to implement it.

Proverbs 8:32 says, "Now listen to me... using wisdom in daily choices, business, and relationships, causes someone to be blessed, [happy, fortunate]. Blessed are those who keep My ways."

Yes, most people do like, may even yearn for, being the recipient of a unique wonder. Of course, don't we want the stallion, the royal crown, the adventure, the Hollywood ending?

The beautiful mystical truth about living in the refuge of the Lord is that even when a person fails, God does not fail. Sampson fell into many sins against Yahweh and his own people, but when his beloved betrayed him, when his eyes were put out, Sampson developed a truer perspective and faith to ask for a final victory in service to the One True God. Even during intense suffering or persecution, the LORD's mercies are new every morning,[16] declares Lamentations. He is the One who brings loving kindnesses over those who love Him and keep His commandments from generation to generation.[17] When we consider the source of this love, these blessings, our adoption, this favor and advantage—it is becoming to experience awe in the wonder of the

Lord God, the Creator. He is the continuing Artist of heaven and Earth. Experiencing a relationship with this kind of God can overwhelm.

> So, what about the times of David's life when he was disguised and fleeing for his life from King Saul?[18]
> What about Job when he fell in one day from being the father of the most beautiful children in the land, the most prosperous rancher, to being childless, a body sick with boils, with a wife who taunted him to curse God and die?[19]
> What about the crucible Queen Esther found herself in having to choose whether to disclose the truth of the evil nature of her all-powerful king's best friend, risking her neck to try to change the law in effect against her race?[20]
> What about poor Joseph who was betrayed by his brothers, sold into slavery in a heathen nation, falsely accused by Potiphar's wife, and left to rot in prison?[21]
> What about the childless Hannah and Rachael when the only thing that mattered for women in their culture was to have children?[22]
> What about falsely accused Daniel sent to punishment in the lion's den,[23] or the three princes in Nebuchadnezzar's kingdom (Babylon) who were sent to a fiery execution?[24]
> What about the apostles in shipwrecks,[25] the beheaded,[26] the crucified,[27] imprisoned,[28] and

all those other unnamed saints who have
passed on from this life to the next?

Were these believers unlucky? Were they unloved?
Unprotected? Unwealthy? Unenviable? Were they
defrauded somehow of God's kindness and promises?

My educated guess is that there is a right answer
hidden in a secret place, but people are often too
emotionally limited by their present experiences and
woes to seek these secrets from the Lord. It is simpler
to pronounce a judgment on God. It is difficult to
believe in the goodness of God or wait for the love of
God to be revealed when we encounter emotional
things that seem unfair. It is difficult to practice trust
in God. It is hard to continue to defer to His honor or
follow where He leads in the middle of great loss.

Nevertheless. . . God will not stop guiding and
intervening in human affairs until the day of the Lord.
The word sanctification means that He is personally
working within you to do His will and good pleasure.
Philippians 2:13 indicates that God even changes our
intentions to want to do things of glory in alignment
with His will. He clothes us with royal clothing for our
life of ashes. He reinvents the wheel. He comforts. He
absolves. Why not grab onto this language and hold
on for dear life?

Consider what happened to Jacob's blessing of
Joseph's two sons in Genesis 48:13–14 when one hand
crossed over, passed over, the head of the elder child
and placed itself on the head of the younger child. Did

that act, those words, take effect? There is evidence that it did and evidence that it didn't. Are you willing to ask for wisdom and truth on the issue before asserting your opinion? Finding out whether there are inherited powers in the blessings invoked of God's people to others may make the wonder of your writing broader. Write about spiritual wonders to your generation and to your children.

In the events of Joseph's life, those unlikely movements from abandonment to unjust punishment to ruler... did God intervene? Let me ask you whether you believe that God has promised rewards for certain action or inaction we take in this world? Beyond God's common grace, and His covenanted mercy for faith, are there special rewards and natural consequences from God?

Joseph's only security in life was his fidelity to God. Did God reward Joseph's tenacious faith? He blessed Joseph's personal life, and through him, he saved the whole nation.[29] How about the Moabitess when she chose the family of God over her natural family deciding to care for her mother-in-law in a foreign land? From loss and grief to favor and belonging with Boaz' household, Ruth leapt, and into the line of Jesus.[30] David's persecution by the anointed king of Israel molded him into the legendary leader who was labeled, "the man after God's own heart."[31]

Many of God's blessings do not come without passages of suffering.

The provincial orphaned Esther being guided by Mordecai, and watched over even when she became queen, learned that her real jurisdiction and power, her real authority came from her Lord God. Not from her husband the king or even from the new laws established in the land.[32]

Deborah, the studious judge who listened to God, became the commander of an army. She was the highly unlikely winner, but she and another unlikely woman, Jael, cast off their persecutors' rampages of countrymen by showing courageous faith.[33]

Christians are given a holy language of authority from the Lord: a language of blessing, wisdom, righteousness, music, transcendental favor, rewards from on high for the making good decisions. Proverbs 8:34 says, "How blessed, [happy, fortunate and to be envied] is the one who listens to me, watching daily at my gates, waiting at the posts of my doors." Learning to use wisdom is not portrayed as an instantaneous process, but a watching, listening, and waiting-to-use-when-needed process.

Unmerited love and courage is not offered to a select group, but to anyone who will be bothered by God. Compassion and miracles too are wonders infused into human events so that it can be known that God answers prayer.

The Biblical language of our forefathers is not just Christianese. Believers are given Biblical terminology that is full of God's own authority, His skill, and it is full of mystique. Esther and Deborah learned to know

God's joy as their own strength. Faith is the substance
of things hoped for, the evidence of things not seen.[34]
His Word is transformative in power. It lives to be
accessed by us should we choose to accept this
mission.

"When I consider the work of Your fingers, the
moon and the stars, what is man that You are mindful
of him?" Here in Psalm 8:3–4, the marveling of the
psalm writer is expressed. What is man that You are
mindful of him? Psalm 33 shows us something far
better than magic, the poetry of God's breath
exhaling:

"By the word of the LORD the heavens were
made, their starry host by the breath of his mouth. He
gathers the waters of the sea into jars; he puts the
deep into storehouses. Let all the earth fear the
LORD; let all the people of the world revere him. For
he spoke, and it came to be; he commanded, and it
stood firm." Can you imagine it happening? Psalm 33
continues, "The plans of the LORD stand firm forever,
the purposes of his heart through all generations.
Blessed is the nation whose God is the LORD."[35]

After reading this chapter, I hope it has become
more clear that a blessing is only as good as its source.
He chose His people for *His own inheritance*, and to
that end, He will work miracles, marvels, and
wonders.

You may only find one significant connection to
an artist, musician, writer, or film-maker in your
whole life.

Nurture that one. Give honor to whom honor is due. When you support a clever artist, you actively return real appreciation by your own clever deeds. You are personally recognizing the living spirit of God inside the maker-creator. You are actively returning thanks to the Creator-God for that gift being expressed. You are also acknowledging the person who emulates the Creator.

Rule 8: NURTURE. Nurture someone's vision.

Exercise: Toss some bread upon the water. In other words, name one person whom you might encourage and list how you will be intentional in helping them.

WRITE DOWN ONE NAME YOU MAY HELP:

WRITE ONE PROJECT TO HELP WITH:

CHOOSE A HELPING IDEA FROM THIS LIST:
Start or Join a Support Group for creatives
Offer Venue for an Art Show
Introduce_____ to
_____
Set up a Fund in an Organization or Church for Artists
Speak to a Group about Creativity
Start a Social Media Campaign for a project
Organize a Book Lunch for a Debut Author. Tell Everyone to write a Four or Five-Star Review
Give a Helpful Book to a Maker or Creator
Facilitate a Creator's Bible Study
Create a Business Plan for a Creative
Offer to Format or Edit a Poster, Manuscript, or Song
Start an Annual Marketing Fair or Conference
Put an Creative Idea in a Leader's Ear and Offer to Help it Make it Happen
Teach Someone to Design a Website for Themselves

9

NOT ALL ART IS FOR ALL SOULS

Let's admit it. Media appeals to the senses. Food is sensual. Earth is sensual. Humans are sensual. Marriage is a sacred, sensual and sexual phase in life for many. It is an ordinance of Christianity in all denominations and practices. Sexuality inside and outside of marriage is offered for models of discussion throughout Scripture. May we presume that God created sensuality and sexuality?

May we also presume that it is only the perversions of sexuality that are outside the limits of Scripture and nature - such as improper priorities, using people, misappropriating sensuality, or indiscretions of timing or place - which indicate rebelliousness? Is this what separates good sensuality from bad?

Experiencing the sensual is implicit to being human, the physiology created by the Creator. Even the most fundamental of us cannot escape the infusion of beauty in life. While type-written expressions of sensuality in God's Word have an important place, they are not always the fullest expression for every adult experience. God's own purpose is not always expressed best in verbal discourse or written letters when foreplay and intercourse are purposed. There. I said it. The Song of Solomon is preserved in the canon of the Holy Bible to endorse the mysteries of sexuality, sensuality, and civil matrimony.

To you having ears, hear this.

ENJOY!

It is improper to erase all representations of something that God purposely included for our abundance. In fact, God endorses the use of sensuality in music while at the same time He complains, "Look at that! You are like a sensual song that everyone loves to hear, but nobody really obeys or listens to for application of the meaning!"[36]

When I was a single professional, another gal who is a lovely friend, wrote a song for me lifted from this verse in Zephaniah. Here is the image of a warrior-lover singing over his beloved in Zephaniah 3:5 and 17: "The LORD is righteous within her; He will do no injustice."[...]"God, The LORD is with you, the Mighty Warrior who saves. He will take great delight in you; in His love He will no longer rebuke you, but will rejoice over you with singing." It is still a precious gift to remember that the warrior-God takes such great delight in me so as to sing over me in love. What a Biblical-sensual image!

The LORD also chooses to use the marital image as apropos to His love toward all who have been jilted, betrayed, or abandoned. "It will no longer be said to you, 'Forsaken,' nor to your land will it any longer be said, 'Desolate'; but you will be called, 'Beautiful! My delight is in her,' And your land, 'Married'; For the LORD delights in you, and to Him your land will be married. For as a young man marries a virgin, so will your God marry you; and as the bridegroom rejoices over the bride, so your God will rejoice over you" Isaiah 62:4–5 (NASB).

Psalm 19:5 also personifies the created sun, "which is as a bridegroom coming out of his chamber; like a champion rejoicing to run his course. ...and nothing is hidden from its heat." There is profound joy and passion in this image of an eager and faithful bridegroom created in this psalm for us (NIV).

And, we are to have a similar zeal (passion) for the fellowship of the LORD, seeking intimacy with Him in all we do, greeting Him as with a kiss of delight,[37] lest His anger is roused for our lack of desire for Him. In repenting, we are not to fake it, but be passionate about it.[38] The apostle Paul indicated that we can be zealous spiritually but *misdirected*: "For I testify about them that they are zealous for God, but not on the basis of knowledge. Because they were ignorant of God's righteousness and sought to establish their own, they did not submit to God's righteousness."[39]

Attempting to establish ourselves without God's means is a form of creating a graven image. Whatever we manage to build is in vain. "Unless the LORD builds the house, they labor in vain that build it; unless the LORD guards the city, the watchman keeps awake in vain. It is vain for you to rise up early, to retire late, to eat the bread of painful labors; for He gives to His beloved even in his sleep."[40]

A creative watchfully calculates work for a target audience, and decides whether a group should be included or excluded while crafting the aim of a scene. We work for the LORD, not as people pleasers.

Not all art, however, is intended for all ears and eyes. Not all art is intended for every phase of life. Not all sensual things are intended for holy places.

Isaiah's dictation of God's complaint against the church said, "Who is trampling contempt into my courts? Your incense is detestable to me! Your feasts and festivals and even your solemn liturgies I hate with all my Being."[41] This was because the artistry of religious worship was all fluff without anyone dispensing true religious practices by caring for orphans and widows (powerless and marginalized). Make *faithful* art, which is art that does not promote or permit fraudulent acts of worship.

GOOD IN LOVE

We know that reading "Adam knew Eve" is not the same thing as experiencing the relational act personally or modeling it with another person for theater or writing a scene from imagination and purposeful parameters. Scripture writers often used veiled references. Though the Bible is a guide meant for all phases of life, not all age groups should be exposed to the facts of sexuality. Even movies have ratings. The Internet has parental controls.

Common sense informs us that our aims, our parameters, and our reasons for creating scenes with sexual content should be carefully evaluated.

I recently saw a sign that read in bold letters, "GOD LOVES SEX!" It made me smile. It was an advertisement for a seminar about freeing people from the debilitating and deconstructive lifestyle of pornography.

How many religious people have been trained to believe that sensuality, games, jokes, media, music, and books are not from the LORD? The reasoning goes like this: if media doesn't include scriptures or apologetics, if it doesn't depict the ideal image having tied up all the loose tailings, if Christianese or King James speech or models of evangelism fail to control the art, then how can that art be *good* for us? Holy? How could it be *from* the LORD's hand?

In order to call it Christian, don't we have to interject the ideal back into the picture? Is it safe to speak about conflicting passions, genitals, and temptations within a church community? What good can come of admitting a movie stirred a beautiful response or a practical violent or sexual question?

Nevertheless, we must recognize contexts that are appropriate and inappropriate to address things pertaining to humanity within the Kingdom of God. And, sexuality must always be within the context of protecting purity and holiness.

Some critics are hypervigilant, however, they only look to the familiar religious lingo. This rhetoric traps us in guilt simply for being human. Hyper-vigilance lacks godly imagination and good research. It operates outside of the inspiration of God's intent. Don't forget that medical journals and certain aspects of counseling require accurate descriptions or depictions of bodies. If there is an opportunity to glorify God through awkward subjects, do what Ephesians 5:16 advises:

> "Be careful how you live. Don't live like fools, but like those who are wise. Make the most of every opportunity in these evil days. Don't act thoughtlessly, but understand what the LORD wants you to do." (NLT)

We'd like to rise above the common man by citing John 3:16 and First Corinthians 13 as the difference between the agape love and other forms of love often experienced in songs, movies, and other forms of art. Isn't agape higher love?

In reality, agape in the original Greek language simply meant love.[42] And all love is invented by God for God and for our good.

God in Christ is higher love becoming human. His transcendence wasn't to aspire, but to reach down.

Without human love for others (horizontal), it is impossible to please Him (vertical). If an expression or feeling is "love," (even sexual *eros* love) it is a form of *agape*. God created a variety of loves for a variety of human relationships. If God didn't feel the need to spell out every nuance of love or aspect of doctrine about Himself and His world, why take it upon ourselves to imperialize, censor, label, and critique things we should only be sharing and gratefully enjoying in its proper setting, or discussing or pondering for a purpose?

Does this sound like a slippery slope? But, I am not saying that all sex is an act of love. Sex can be an expression of love, or it can express rage, unholy self-indulgence, or a mental illness. Nor am I advocating that church leaders allow any form of sexual touches or sexual images inside the place of worship used as holy to God. Yes, teachers should warn about lust and exploitation.

Counselors should teach, preachers should preach, parents should parent, and friends should warn! I'm asking, nevertheless, that Christians also acknowledge that sensuality is sacred in many forms and sex acts are meant for marriage.

Portrayal of sexual subjects in an artistic work should clearly indicate that spousal acts are of the good hand of God.[43] God's rules are either being heeded, or perverted, and the artist should indicate that a blessing of life is the reward, or that the choice of perversion is leading to the curse of destruction.

When sensuality is misplaced or fails to mimic the godly model, it is a shade off of the image. God isn't surprised since He's well aware that sin has entered His world. Though He hates the sin, He loves the sinner.

A sensual scene doesn't always have to be clipped away, but graphic sex can lead to sin. Our hearts were designed to bear witness to the truths lying conflicted together. God's law is written on our souls. The Holy Spirit is alive and well to correct and inform. It lies within our grasp to understand when violence is perverse and war is evil, and also when necessity demands the story of it.

When it is determined whether a scene stays or gets clipped, the decision may require some additional instruction and a boundary from Scripture or natural, common sense. As adults, we don't always have to spin the mysterious wonder enjoyed by our senses with a "but...".

Find the good and exploit it for good. Even a bad example is an example. BE VIGILANT. There is creative good to be found in awkward situations. King Solomon made a list to emphasize that there is a time and a place for everything under heaven.[44]

Learning to wield the sensuality tool is to grow up and study hard. Develop personal character - as a creative. *Remember righteous thinking and righteous input is ingenious and life-giving.* Pray without ceasing. Envision redemption. Envision the light going on and spiritual muscles being flexed.

Sensual scenes may be used to cast a warning sign. In all art, something of God and something profound can be collected on a shelf of the soul, but not all media is worth it. Do yourself a favor. Let the voice of the Living Word inform the boundaries of your art.

IMAGES FOR SELF-GLORY OR GOD'S GLORY

I did some valuable research in Scripture for guidance relative to images that provoke the senses. It became obvious that sensuous images move the soul toward the Creator or against Him. Here is what I discovered.

One of the most misunderstood of the ten commandments is this: "You shall have no other gods before or besides Me. You shall not make for yourself a graven image in the form of anything in heaven above or on the earth beneath or in the waters below. You shall not bow down to them or worship them; for I, the LORD your God, am a jealous God, punishing the children for the sin of the parents to the third and fourth generation of those who hate me."[45]

What is a "graven image," pray tell?

This term is used with "molten image" in Hosea 11:2, saying, "They sacrificed to Baalim, and burned incense to graven images." Bishop Horsley explains, "...to spread, or cover all over, either by pouring forth a substance in fusion, or in spreading a cloth over or before, or by hammering on metalline plates."[46]

This covering over of God's creativity describes the use of a crafter for deceptive purposes. The use gains a serious, personal liability in Deuteronomy 27:15, which forewarns us: "Anyone will be cursed who makes an idol or statue and secretly sets it up, because the LORD hates [detests] the idols people make [the work of the hand of an artisan; De.5:8–10; Ex. 34:17; Is. 44:9–20]. Then all the people will say, 'Amen!'"

The significance of "a graven image," is that which is not living art, from the LORD, but that which is an expression of one's own pride and passion, planned in secret to serve one's self, obscuring it from the face of the LORD, or His voice, and leading to the grave rather than to living glory.

Habakkuk 2:18–19 says, "What profit is an idol when its maker has shaped it, a metal image, a teacher of lies? For its maker trusts in his own creation when he makes speechless idols! Woe to him who says to a wooden thing, Awake; to a silent stone, Arise! Can this teach? Behold, it is overlaid with gold and silver, and *there is no breath at all in it*" (ESV).

Do you get the feeling that an "idol" is Biblical hyperbole for all kinds of things we glob onto for self-identification other than Christ, and for raising up our standard of living apart from God's provision? "Live for me!" we demand. "Make my life beautiful! Compete for me!"

A graven image can be conceived from personal intellect or another outside influence. It can represent sex, horrors, or deceptively crafted images which cause others to worship that which leaves them empty and without God.

Creatives who craft graven images deny divine providence. They attempt to replace God's will with their own ingenuity.

> "All who make idols are nothing, and the things
> they treasure are worthless. Those who would
> speak up for them are blind; they are ignorant, to
> their own shame. Who shapes a god and casts an
> idol, which can profit nothing?
> People who do that will be put to shame; such
> craftsmen are only human beings.
> Let them all come together and take their stand;
> they will be brought down to terror and shame."
> *Isaiah* 44:9-11 (NIV)

Crafters of graven images seek adoration for themselves. "The sword of these images will even strike her water supply, causing it to dry up. And why? Because the whole land is filled with idols, and the people are madly in love with them."[47]

They create for their own pride of life and greed. *Isaiah* 44:17–18 reads like a powerful promise of holiday commercials equating sleek vehicles and liquor as a quick fix to all that we long for. "From the rest he makes a god, his idol; he bows down to it and worships. He prays to it and says, 'Save me! You are my god!' They know nothing, they understand nothing; their eyes are plastered over so they cannot see, and their minds closed so they cannot understand" (NIV).

It is nonsense not to want to co-create within the expanse of God's living expressions of reality or goodness for His glory because:

"I, the LORD, have called you in righteousness;
I will take hold of your hand.
I will keep you and will make you to be a covenant
for the people
and a light for the Gentiles, to open eyes that are
blind, to free captives from prison
and to release from the dungeon those who sit in
darkness."
Isaiah 42:6–7 (NIV)

To deny the influence of the Creator in our art is to create dead idols. "To whom then will you liken God, or what likeness compare with him? An idol! A craftsman casts it, and a goldsmith overlays it with gold and casts for it silver chains. He who is too impoverished for an offering chooses wood that will not rot; he seeks out a skillful craftsman to set up an idol that will not move."[48]

The LORD has already ordained:
"I am the LORD; that is my name!
I will not yield my glory to another
or my praise to idols."[49]

NAKED I CAME, AND NAKED I'LL GO

In the beginning, physical nakedness—together with spiritual and emotional nakedness—was a state of pure being. "The man and his wife were both naked and were not ashamed." says Genesis 2:25, (NASB). And a baby is born wearing nothing.[50] But, as soon as Adam and Eve broke confidence with God, they felt a need to be clothed. "Then the eyes of both of them were opened, and they knew that they were naked; and they sewed fig leaves together and made themselves loin coverings. He said, "I heard the sound of You in the garden, and I was afraid because I was naked; so I hid myself."[51]

This sudden change in attitude and relationship came about because, "the serpent was more crafty than any other beast of the field that the LORD God had made. He said to the woman, 'Did God actually say, "You shall not eat of any tree in the garden?""[52]

So, through Satan's thread of deception in God's creation, human sexuality—and viewing another's nakedness—became our source of confusion and shame. If you are a crafter in any media, think of God's anger when tempted to craft objects of lust. Objectifying any human being makes a precious soul one-dimensional, an object for the dishonorable intent of others. Soft pornography is found on Internet advertising, on film and book covers, and on billboards everywhere. Don't be any part of it.

By the time the story of Noah rolls around in Genesis 9:23, discovering nakedness in the family has taken a turn. "Then Shem and Japheth took a garment, laid it on both their shoulders, and walked backward and covered the nakedness of their father. Their faces were turned backward, and they did not see their father's nakedness" (ESV). Here we see that covering their father's nakedness caused Noah's sons to be discrete. Honor covers their father's lapse.

Leviticus 18 expounds on the law of God to explain the terms of adultery, fornication, sexuality, and nakedness, "You shall not uncover the nakedness of any relative or lie with them as a spouse. You shall not lie with beast(s) as a spouse. Homosexual acts also are included with these abominations. The chapter is summed up: "You shall therefore keep My statutes and My judgments, and shall not commit *any* of these abominations; *neither* any of your own nation, nor any stranger that passes among you: if you do, the land will spew you out..." (Leviticus 18:30).

Wearing nothing but undergarments in front of others was considered nakedness. When fishing near-naked in a boat, John alerted Peter that Jesus was about, so Peter immediately put on his cloak.[53]

Though there are certainly other secret or private parts, the LORD plainly declared that uncovering the legs and thighs was also nakedness.[54] For this reason, the priests were told to wear breeches to cover these parts under their priestly attire. Musicians who act as musical priests to the LORD and to His people on stage in places of holiness to the LORD need to dress in a beautiful and glorifying manner, without any view of genitals or breasts or in sexually shape-fitted clothing. This includes men and women. It is the Biblical rule regardless of fashion or naïveté.

My point is to learn God's opinion, and fashion your stories to adhere to His values. The dress code for beauty and modesty of all priests ministering in the presence of God, according to Moses in the book of Exodus, were these: "You shall make holy garments for Aaron your brother for glory and for beauty. . . .For Aaron's sons you shall make coats, and girdles, and you shall make bonnets for them, for glory and for beauty. . . .And you shall make them linen breeches *to cover their nakedness;* from the loins even unto the thighs they shall reach: Aaron, and his sons shall wear these when they approach the tabernacle of the congregation, or when they come near to the altar to minister in the holy place; so that they bear no iniquity, and die: it shall be a statute forever to the priest and to his seed after him."[55]

Public nakedness is a Biblical sign of punishment and captivity, *not* freedom or honor.

- Of the destruction of Babylon, he describes their uncovering as part of their undoing saying, "put off your veil, strip off your robe, uncover your legs, pass through the rivers. Your nakedness shall be uncovered, and your disgrace shall be seen."[56] Also predicted of Egypt's captivity.[57]

- Hosea 2:3 shouts, "I will strip her naked as on the day when she was born. She shall be like a wilderness and a desert in her thirst!" (NIV).
- As for a passage in the judgment on Jerusalem, it was written, "I will gather all your lovers with whom you took pleasure, even all those whom you loved and all those whom you hated. So I will gather them against you from every direction and expose your nakedness to them that they may see all your nakedness."[58]

In fact, not all sex or nudity is sensuous. Some aspects of gender are funny, mechanical, and technical; when students learn to paint, photograph, and sculpt the human form, they learn to respect, measure, contour, and mimic the detailed art of our Creator. Copying nudity is required and considered necessary for art education.

A Christian revels in the gift of creativity, and while being thankful for all these blessings, a Christian seeks direction from the Scriptures and asks the Spirit for personal direction in this.

CONSUMERISM ART

Using art to make a living is a perfectly fine way to support yourself. Braun Brush Company is one of America's oldest family-owned industrial brush manufacturers.

From the start, Emanuel Braun, a German immigrant, implemented handmade, quality manufacturing techniques to produce brushes as effective household tools. They became popular. Who doesn't need a variety of brushes, right?

However, at the turn of the century when the industrial revolution started, the factory, like most small manufacturing businesses, fell on hard times. Mass production by machine, whether inferior in quality or not, overwhelmed them. Authors and publishers might relate to the phenomenon.

Again in the 50s, when China got creative and began mass production of common household items to America, Braun could have given up.

Instead, Braun began identifying one person at a time who needed a unique brush. He could still fill that market of one each time he designed a unique brush making his mark up, because the Chinese machines were making multiples for the masses, not unique needs. Finding one-of-a-kind niches, inventing brushes for commercial institutions such as NASA and nuclear plants for cleaning silos, sustained Braun's brush business. Braun understood that not all designs were for all people, so he turned the tables and specialized. Ingenious. Sometimes it isn't the quantities, but the value of rarity. The Braun family members continue to design, craft, and sell brushes in new markets.

Creatives who are fortunate enough to find creative work in the corporate world also need to operate from the center of their spiritual axis to please God above all else.

Marketing and publicity are supportive and creative behind-the-scene middle-man careers.

But, what if your boss asks you to put in the gratuitous sex, or a rape scene, or glorify petty theft *just because*? If you are working purely for financial success, without a higher calling to righteousness, working for consumerism may find you in slavery to sin sitting with your nose in the corner.

Creating anything from the authority of the LOGOS, the life-giving hub, can be a comprehensively risky, often thoughtfully difficult task, in commercial art. The Lord knows that securing the placement of a good job or artistic career means putting a roof over your head. Do you trust the LORD to provide for you, to show you favor if you work to please Him, not sin?

The following figure of speech is a caveat. Presented in Revelation 3 and beginning in verse 14, these are "'the *words* of the Amen, the faithful and true witness, *the beginning of God's creation*. I know your works: you are neither cold nor hot. Would that you were either cold or hot! So, because you are lukewarm, and neither hot nor cold, I will spit you out of my mouth (literally, you make me wretch).[59]

"For you say, 'I am rich, I have prospered, and I need nothing,' not realizing that you are wretched, pitiable, poor, blind, and naked. I counsel you to buy from me gold refined by fire, so that you may be rich, and white garments so that you may clothe yourself and the shame of your nakedness may not be seen, and salve to anoint your eyes, so that you may see".[60]

Here, John, the apostle who is writing, reminds us that the beginning of God's creation is the faithful and true witness through Christ's Word, which is faithful and true from *initial breath* through the *finishing Amen*. We have to make our choice whether to follow the pattern of the faithful and true witness or to serve money, fame and rebellion leading to death. Hot or cold?

To make graven images apart from the Creator's life-giving art—makes you pitiable, poor, blind, and naked. To make sacrifices to purchase the LORD's gold refined by fire leads to living richly, clothed in righteousness and honor, being given healing ointment for physical or spiritual eyes to see.

These are our witnesses. Proverbs 9:6 calls out, "Forsake the foolish, and live; go in the way of understanding!"(KJV).

Rule 9: FIND YOUR AUDIENCE. Not all art is for all people. There are times when one person says, "You may; I may not," or, "You are another man's servant. I'm not to judge you. I am to walk my own path in a pure and circumspect way as God reveals."

10

GOOD HUMOR IS SACRED

Being creative can be a boisterous load of fun! Some, especially in the maker culture, understand good fun. There was, however, a century or two in church history where humor was considered sacrilegious.

Historically, if rectors or ministers wasted their parishioners' time by telling jokes in the pulpit, they were reprimanded or even discharged for desecrating a holy calling.

Maybe there was a point to this. After all, no verse of Scripture instructs good Christians to be silly or to laugh, so a doctrine of good humor may be difficult to pull out of Scripture by chapter and verse.

These days, however, getting the laughter rolling from the pulpit enjoys an allotted time-frame.

I've used a lot of silly words in this essay for the purpose of lighting up some ideas being conveyed.

Does my use of silly technique place my work in a lower form of spiritual communication? Does it fall into the secular box for you rather than into the "sacred speech" box?

Before we pry away the serious teaching and

preaching from lightweight joking or wry and wittiness, we want to consider the importance of cultivating the fruits of the Spirit. Goodwill, love, kindness, graciousness, contentment, redemption, and joy, *all spring from the development of good humor.*[1]

Humor is experienced in the array of animals and animal antics we enjoy. Children also, created by God, make us laugh in their innocence and also in their naughtiness, causing us to be less judgmental and less harsh. Christians are mandated to practice these attributes of good humor. *Besides this,* God created Mark Lowry, Tim Hawkins, Chonda Pierce, Michael Junior, Ken Davis, Taylor Mason, Brad Stine, Rich Praytor, Thor Ramsey, Jeff Allen, and Aaron Wilburn. Have you listened to the song, Roast Beef, by Andy Gullahorn? We can, therefore, absolutely conclude humor is sacred to God. He assumed that we would not have to be supplied with chapter and verse to discover the importance of laughter. Instead, He taught us through His own creativity and example of creation so that we pick up and ingest the ability to mimic His goodwill and good humor through personal experience and natural expression.

I love that God is an entertainer, and when we mimic Him, we become the best lil' entertainers we can be ourselves. Kathy Joy, a humorist, wrote me this note: "Glad to know Shiv-oo-lery isn't dead!" after she read BEING CREATIVE as it was first entitled, WELCOME TO THE SHIVOO!

The Melody of the Mulberries clever novel kept me smiling and chortling all the way through.

Because our Creator's good humor is modeled for all people by His common grace, potentially all people are able to pick up and mimic God in good humor, kindness, gentleness, forbearance, graciousness, joy and love. All the more then, Christians, who are infilled with the Holy Spirit's power and with access to the light of God's written word. The Apostle Paul advocated for remaining in a state of joy at all times when he wrote his letter to the Philippians. In chapter 4, verse 4 he states, "Rejoice in the LORD always, and again, I say rejoice!" Rejoice is the *active voice* of *being full of joy*. Paul's mandate to those who are already full of love and knowledge? Hey! Put some notes of happiness into your hearts at all times because of Who the LORD is. Rejoice means, "ACTIVATE JOY, PEOPLE! Recycle it. Again!"

And because we have confidence in the risen Savior, Who has promised us many benefits in eternal life, shouldn't we mimic His ironic patience, entertaining goodness, and merriment in our every action and reaction? Proverbs 17:22 clearly equates a merry heart to good (and needed) medicine, using a spice of humor to describe the opposite. A broken spirit tends to dry up the bones.

PRAY FOR BUOYANCY

You cannot manufacture joy. It is a divine gift that we

must submit to, and one that we typically experience when we remain in the LORD's fellowship. When David was severely disciplined for his theft, adultery, and murder, he repented and then prayed, "Restore to me the joy of Your salvation!"[2] If you lack joy, ask the LORD to open the eyes of your heart. These are our marching orders: *find God's good humor.*

Find the exclamation point.

You may have already discovered that sometimes, incredible amounts of creativity are required to produce buoyancy in conflict. What did the Puritans do without television, radio, and cell phones? Maybe they had lively parties with debates, singing and playing instruments, logging uses for medicinal herbs, creating educational material, cooking for groups, planting, harvesting, reading, developing businesses, quilting, writing, storytelling, and reciting. I'm not sure if they danced, but many Christian communities do.

We learn from tragedy, epic or otherwise, but tragedy is a genre of literature—believe it or not—which is considered entertainment. One of the fruits of the Spirit is longsuffering.[3] How can anyone suffer for a long while without some fits of humor to prop them up? Humor is absolutely necessary to human survival, and that is why the Creator gave some to each of us.

When I met my husband, I discovered one of the most delightful senses of humor ever to cross my landscape. I fell in love with him. Gratefully! I had been too serious for way too long. Recently, he told me an old story about how hungry hospital staff used to steal left-over breakfast items, the "safe" ones, from the top of the trash barrel to eat during the morning break. As an aide, my husband arrived to scavenge, however, it was just after the coffee grounds had been tossed on top of a plate of bacon. What did he do? He did what any low paid, hungry man would do. He washed off the bacon and re-plated it. As he carried his cache into the lounge, a nurse spied him. "I hope you're planning to share that," she said. He shared it . . .in all good humor. My husband confessed recently to that nurse for a laugh about the old days— for bonding. For human cheer.

What a gracious gift God gives us when He brings us funny people and stories of situations like that. Light-hearted communication can bring us joy. I think God enjoys silly human jokes.

Notwithstanding the finer gifts of friends, family, and spouses, most of us go through rifts of weeping from loneliness or deserts from lack of attention for long periods, not feeling acknowledged or special to anyone. I go through these myself. During one of these times, someone who barely knew me called me up to pray with me over the phone. The prayer consisted of thanking and praising God for His glistening, shimmering wings laying over me like skin. I was hooked. The prayer blessed God for seeing my fortitude as *exquisite*. I began to tremble and tears began to drip down my face. Why? Because of the perfect pairing of image and words, I grasped that God knew that I needed to know this. He was covering me. He had made me primarily for Himself and I belonged to Him. That although I think of applying the term "exquisite" to someone, it is generally to a finely chiseled form. So, what I heard was God's gracious story of love for me. That He regarded my heart's intent in any fashion, personalized this notion. For two days I soaked up being delighted in by the LORD. I was delighting in the LORD's presence. To know God's presence to any degree as I move through moments of a common day is my uncommon delight. I want to walk with the LORD, my Creator. Is this your desire too? Do you inquire of Him as you are walking, driving, singing, or talking? Do you return thanks to Him?

We can find delight in anything having to do with the LORD or His purposes. I realized recently that often my first reaction to incompetency, or to being slighted, or to seeing sin taking hold, is anger. While there is a reasonable reaction of anger to sin, in order to change someone's mind, I needed to access the power of God's delightful forbearance in wisdom. I have a long way to go in practicing the fly catching trade by using honey as opposed to vinegar.

Even the difference between a wise student and a fool can be depicted in humor. What does foolishness look like, something foul in a punchbowl? Maybe you can write a few lines on a page about someone you know who is wasting life, or draw an image of someone wrapped up in the seduction of false answers, false advertising.

Now,
> hum
>> a melody of
>>> intervals and rhythms
>>>> to indicate foolishness.

If you don't wish to end on that note, try describing a character of meekness in action. Do you see humility in an employee, kindness where it is unlikely? Make note of it in a safe card file for a character you may utilize in a later bit of ingenuity. A fun case can be made for all creativity, all flow of consciousness, and all problem-solving avenues in business. When creatives work with the Creator and not against His priorities, we fall into step. Stay curious. Playfully ask and occasionally copy His own shocking sense of surprise.

Rule 10: ENJOY the ride! Mimic God's secrets and playfulness in your own interpretative life.

TRY TO MAKE A COMPREHENSIVE LIST

OF THE KINDS OF HUMOR THAT ARE

AVAILABLE FOR USE IN YOUR WRITING

OR OTHER ART.

11.

ON A WING AND A PRAYER

I watched the pair of finches in my bird cage for months. They built a nest and laid some eggs, but nothing ever cracked open. One day, I took the cage out to the front porch, and opened the door to clean it out. One of the pretty yellow birds flew out of the opening and into a nearby tree. Plopping onto the chair incredulous at my stupidity, and worried about how the house finch would fare in the upcoming Colorado winter, I sat stunned for some time. Then, I let the other finch go.

Sometimes, in writing, you change one detail that opens up a new window for a character's growth, a relationship, a past, or the future. When one bird flies out the window, another bird follows. That's the way creativity goes.

In these pages, I have made suggestions for observing rules to create by. Yet, here is a puzzle: If you look closely, you will discover that the rules create natural conflict within themselves.

How do you improvise and follow guidelines? How do you insert yourself and accept credit if everything really stems from the Creator? How do you communicate by inuendo if you don't put labels on things in a language understood? How are you not lost if you are wandering? How do you adhere to ancient rules of geography, nature, science, law, and grammar while producing a worthy news item, fresh-faced? How do you create a frame of evil if you are writing or painting for redemption? Did God create both day and night?

Adding and subtracting, opening windows and closing doors, this is where wisdom comes in.

This is where we all learn that real art comes from the heart. Knowledge is learning new things. Wisdom is learning how to show what you know in the right settings. It isn't enough to speak a word, but to speak a word with an added gift of inspiration.

Josiah DeGraaf, writer of The Chronicles of Morshan, said it on his Facebook page this way: "I think the reason many modern Christian stories fail is because they misunderstand why stories affect people the way that they do."

"—Frankenstein shows the dangers of playing God, not by scolding the readers not to do this, but by showing readers how much grief comes from doing so.

"—The Odyssey critiques the Greek idolization of fame, not by several long soliloquys about the problems of fame, but by haunting visual images of the vanity of the pursuit of fame (the underworld) and by Odysseus' own example (choosing family over fame).

"—Crime and Punishment rejects nihilism, not with a one-sided debate between a nihilist and a Christian, but by simply showing the depressing nature of the nihilist life.

"—The Divine Comedy gets the closest to breaking this rule, but even here the most powerful bits (the punishments in Hell, the trials of Purgatory, and the symbols of Heaven—chief of all the Empyrean Rose) are not rational arguments but verbal images meant to stir our emotions around "the love that moves the sun, and moon, and all the other stars.'"

DeGraaf says, "The best stories aren't the ones that use robust, rational arguments to make their case. There's a place for those in non-fiction, but across the past several millennia, the best works of literature have consistently influenced their readers through their emotions, not their reason.

"All these works use rational arguments, but they use them to support the stronger emotional 'arguments' they're making by use of powerful examples. Because while rational arguments work great in non-fiction, fiction is (largely) the realm of emotions. This is why books like Twilight sell. As abusive as these books may be to intellectual thought, they capitalize on the power of fiction to connect with emotions, and they sell millions.

"In contrast to this is the Christian story market, where most of the story's message is delivered in cliched direct arguments meant to appeal to the reader/viewer's rational side. Presumably because their creators think faith in Christ is a purely rational decision." (I know this is a hotly-debated topic, but I suggest conversion is more holistic than that.)

"If Christian storytelling is going to become great again, Christian storytellers need to write with both a more holistic view of humanity in mind—and a view that understands why emotions are integral to storytelling."

Wisdom is the original seed of creativity. The Creative Holy Spirit is eager to be our guide.

We have our imagination and the light of the living Word of God flowing through this world, through history, and through our very own world.

We have all things natural created before we knew how to scribble out a leaf etching in kindergarten. God also gives us noses for spices, observation skills, light and shade, tools for architecture with which to complement or enhance the natural, and also tools to accurately represent the deeds of the devil. For each, there is a purpose. "The purposes of a person's heart are deep waters, but one who has insight draws them out," wrote the scribe in Proverbs 20:5. In your passionate zeal for God and for art, the understated can sometimes be the most powerful image to paint.

THE ART OF WANDERING

Instead of becoming the next contestant on American Idol or America's Got Talent, my phases of creative wrestling taught me to know the Lord better. I also became a better wife, friend, and mentor. I became an author and content editor at Capture Books. Enjoying privacy and working hard behind the scenes fit my lifestyle better. I also found deeply personal treasures. Sacred treasures that I only share in specific circumstances.

CREATING A LIFE WORTH LIVING describes the phases that many creatives transition through. This book helped me to understand my varied interests were legitimate.

Some of my more artful phases included buying dilapidated houses and designing new renovations over the top of them, poetry, of course, faux-finishing walls and furniture, running a retreat for Christian artists and writers, songwriting, creating may publicity pieces, formatting children's books, and making up stories of my own.

All the while, my husband has preferred to stay put in whatever house we lived in at the time and go lurking through the hills on weekends. Probably blowing off steam. Maybe escaping sawdust.

Having pieces falling out, I'm here to say, leaves you with the core of what matters to you.

Pieces falling out can be the way to learn understanding of each other where one partner in a marriage is a creative and the other is anchored to the practicalities of a job and a prayerful hike in the woods every couple of weeks.

Conflict presents opportunities to find creative options for each-your-own life goals. Eventually, I learned to see the benefits of being married to someone so different to me. He was my rock. I was his wingspan. We needed each other.

Don't we all have to learn the flexibility of backing down, and recalculation? Everyone who achieves anything knows that creativity is a necessary skill to finding a way around life's stumbling stones if we intend to stake a real claim somewhere.

The house, we've chosen to remain in, hears our more forthright conversations. My husband and I renovated our home to include space for my artistic lifestyle, and now we are both more in love with each other for accepting all of these struggles as healthy and good life processes.

The art of wandering is in the practice of medicine and law. Why would we not think wandering is required in faith and creativity? We have Abraham, Sarah and Lot wandering, Moses wandered and led the whole nation of Israel into the desert, Jacob ran and wandered, David wandered with a band of mighty men into hiding with an enemy king. Orphaned Esther wandered into the palace to save her people, Ruth wandered after her mother-in-law. Jonah wandered. If you don't believe it, read the book of the bitter Jonah. God's prerogative was to go easy on terrorists and play practical jokes on the one who pouted about it, about being sent to warn them.

Our most semiotic book of the Bible is the conclusive book of Revelation, which wanders through images, prophecies and icons. Let's trust that flow of consciousness as God's gift to each of us, wondering as we wander out under the stars. Mary and Joseph wandered to Egypt. Jesus and John, like Elijah, wandered in the desert. Can artists say Amen to wandering and wondering?

In Revelation chapter 3, we find a key as to why Christians use the word, "Amen," to agree with a spiritual teaching, revelation, or preaching. Do we get that we are actually invoking the person of God? The Apostle John writes in revelations given to him through God, "To the angel of the church in Laodicea write: These are the words of the Amen, the faithful and true Witness, the Originator and Ruler of God's creation..." *What?*

Turning this phrase onto itself, John personifies the Amen as the Originator and continuing Ruler of God's creation! Who or what is the *Amen*? The Amen is the faithful and true Witness. *Who is this Witness?* Once again, we are approached with the incarnation of a word. "I am the Alpha and Omega, the beginning and the end of the Greek alphabet," says the Logos, the Christ, who personally appears with His reward.) "Behold, I am coming quickly, and My reward is with Me, to give to each person according to what he has done. I am the Alpha and the Omega, the First and the Last, the Beginning and the End." He tells us clearly that He is the ongoing creative revelation, the ongoing persuasion, the LOGOS. "Blessed are those who wash their robes, so that they may have the right to the tree of life and may enter the city by its gates..."[4]

So many images and symbols are used in John's flow of consciousness. Although we may not understand anything completely, John is able to communicate with us, the reader (listener), that because Jesus Christ is not only the beginning, but also the ending for us, we can be actively seeking our reward in Him. To enter the city, to access the tree of life, we should be soaping, bleaching, soaking, pounding, and wringing our robes to ready ourselves for this reward... in Christ!

The mission to be profound, pithy, pertinent and plucky is uniquely processed by each creative.

Although we need to help eradicate filth and disease as a surgeon goes about it, and as the warning of the angel goes to the Church of Laodicea in this Revelation, at the same time we treat ourselves to the depth of tenderness found in the Lamb's complete sacrifice for us.

There are many dark sayings of the wise, just as Grimm and Aesop and Jonah knew, as the writers of Scripture depicted the good with the bad, and as many writers today understand.

"This is the proverb of Solomon, the son of David, king of Israel; To know wisdom and instruction; to perceive the words of understanding; To receive the instruction of wisdom, justice, and judgment, and equity. To give subtlety to the simple, to the young person knowledge and discretion. Someone wise will hear, and will increase in learning; and someone of understanding shall attain to the standard of wise counsels: understanding a proverb, and the interpretation of it; the words of the wise, and their dark sayings. The fear of the LORD is the beginning of knowledge: *but* fools despise wisdom and instruction."[5] Don't try to sugarcoat the LORD or His wanderings with the aim of getting quick wisdom for the applause of others. Tell the colorful truth - where appropriate - so help you God.

Creatives, mentors, nurturers, and performers provide cross woven values to others. They honor their Father–Creator when they participate in this holy and sanctified calling, practicing good stewardship and development of their gifts. Second Corinthians 9:15 exclaims, "Thanks be to God for His indescribable, inexplicable gift, too wonderful for words!" In this context I also find my final blessing to you as my reader:

"As it is written: 'He has scattered abroad His gifts to the poor; His righteousness endures forever.' Now He who supplies seed to the sower and bread for food will supply and multiply your store of seed and will increase the harvest of your righteousness. You will be enriched in every way to be generous on every occasion, and your giving through us will produce thanksgiving to God. For this ministry of service is not only supplying the needs of the saints, but is also overflowing in many expressions of thanksgiving to God. Because of the proof this ministry provides, the saints will glorify God for your obedient confession of the gospel of Christ, and for the generosity of your contribution to them and to all the others. And their prayers for you will express their affection for you, *because of the surpassing grace God has given you."* [6]

In order to mimic His priorities in playing this game, we practice recognizing the Giver whenever we see, hear, smell, touch or otherwise experience life's gifts.

We give props to the LORD as we cultivate our resources in the land He has given us.[7] We need margins of waiting things out, or waiting for God to move. We rest and explore. We intentionally converse about what we've discovered. We read and write, memorize, act, and sing. We don't always understand why something artistically absolutely works or just doesn't work at all. Accept the mystery. We work hard, share the work with others, focus on detail, and observe the rules of the Creator's game because it is, after all, His game. He invented it.

Think of the rules as *invitations*. Praise Him with noise and gongs and loud Amens! Praise Him with the tinkling bells and harps. Bow down and worship Him. Kiss the Son, lest He be angry as a lover for being ignored. *Participate in your blessings.* Use your full physiological being in big expressions and small.

Creatives practice art as a lawyer practices law, as a doctor practices medicine. Yet, the secret stays the same. "The fear of the LORD is the beginning of wisdom: and the knowledge of the holy is understanding."[8] The LORD invites you to measure your artistic steps so that you may keep learning more of what this means to your life and your craft.

When we mimic God's own creative priorities, profound reasoning, and ironic humor, we are tottering after Him hard, just like a child shadows a parent. Psalm 139:17 says He speaks personally to you. So revel in your unique communications from Him and your set of skills inherited from your Creator.

Cultivate education. Cultivate laughter. Cultivate nutritious food. Cultivate respect for others. Cultivate unity in God's children. Cultivate financial codes of conduct. Cultivate imagination and creativity. Cultivate healthy boundaries.

Cultivate responsibility. Cultivate praise.

Practice worship on a daily basis. Begin and end your days with praise.

The LOGOS is sharing His gifts with you. Now,

MAY THE AXIS OF GOD'S EXPANSIVE REVELATION FLY YOUR WHEELS!

GO!

CREATE SOMETHING!

ABOUT THE AUTHOR

Laura Bartnick has managed Capture Books since 2015. She graduated with a degree in Bible and Music from Montana Bible College and then earned a B.A. in Contemporary Composition at Colorado Christian University. She finished her education in paralegal studies at Denver Paralegal Institute.

The author of the devotional, Every Day Bride (1998), she additionally authored two other awarded books under pen names. Her work has been published in several magazines and journals including The Door, Shofar, and Inklings. She currently writes for fun and to do business for Capture Books authors.

If you have something to say about this book, please make comments to your book club, in classrooms, and to your friends privately. If you really want to stir it up, we'll read about it on Amazon, Goodreads, and in your social networks. We'll thank you for your honesty.

For more remarkable books, visit www.BooksForBondingHearts.com

_____

CHAPTER ENDNOTES

CHAPTER 1: FIRST MEANS PRIORITY
[1] I credit Robin Bownes, at Robin B Creative, www.Bownes.co.za, with providing to me the ancient Greek definition of Logos used in this book.
[2] "Logos," Logos, Wikipedia, last modified on December 9, 2019, https://en.wikipedia.org/wiki/Logos.
[3] Eph. 5:23 New King James Version
[4] Ps. 98:9.
[5] 1 Cor. 10:31.
[6] Gen. 1:1.
[7] Gen. 1:1.
[8] John 3:16.
[9] Gen. 1:26 Easy-to-Read Version.
[10] Gen. 3:7 Berean Study Bible.
[11] Gen. 3:23–24.
[12] Lev. 1–27.
[13] Matt. 11:5;.
[14] "Benedictine-Values," MaterChristi, last modified 2019, materchristi.edu.au/benedictine-values.
[15] Hosea 1:2.
[16] Exod. 13:2; 22:29–31; 34:19.
[17] Deut. 21:15–17.
[18] Exod. 34:19.
[19] Gen. 27:1–29 BSB.
[20] Gen. 48:13–22.
[21] Gen. 35:22; 49:1–4.
[22] Rom. 8:29.
[23] 1 Cor. 15:20.
[24] 1 Cor. 15:52.
[25] N. T. Wright, "How Can The Bible Be Authoritative?," *Vox Evangelica* 21 (1991), p.18.
[26] "Science", Anatomy in Leonardo da Vinci., N.P., https://www.leonardo-da-vinci.ch/science.
[27] Sue Bender, *Plain and Simple: A Woman's Journey to the Amish*, (New York: HarperCollins Publishers, 1991), 89.
[28] Bender, 141.
[29] Matt. 4:1–11.

[30] Exod. 2:15–21.
[31] Matt. 4:1–4.
[32] Exod. 2:15–21; 3:1–Deut. 4:5. These passages of Moses' life tell of how he met and married his wife, and how he became the leader God intended him to be leading Israel from captivity and later provided Israel with God's own instruction on how to live.

[33] W. L. Walker, "Cunning" In *The International Standard Bible Encyclopedia*, edited by James Orr, N.P.,1915. http://classic.studylight.org/enc/isb/view.cgi?number=T2446.
[34] Col. 1:9–10.

CHAPTER 2: ACKNOWLEDGE THE CREATOR

[1] Prov, 3:6 New King James Version.
[2] Michael Hodgin, *1001 More Humorous Illustrations for Public Speaking: Fresh, Timely, and Compelling Illustrations for Preachers, Teachers, and Speakers*, (Grand Rapids: Zondervan Publishing House, 1998), 207.
[3] Matt. 27:45–51.
[4] Gal. 6:7.
[5] Hab. 1:12–13.
[6] Ps. 103:12.
[7] 1 Pet. 5:8.
[8] John 10:10 NKJV.
[9] Gen. 3:1–7.
[10] Ezek. 28; Isa. 14:12–14.
[11] 1 Pet. 5:8—9 Berean Study Bible.
[12] Bob Dylan, *Gotta Serve Somebody*, (Sheffield: Muscle Shoals Sound Studios, 1979), https://genius.com/Bob-dylan-gotta-serve-somebody-lyrics.
[13] Isa. 3:8.
[14] Rom. 1:21 English Standard Version.
[15] Bob Deffinbaugh, "The Glory of God (Romans 8:30)," Bible.org, August 18, 2004, https://bible.org/seriespage/19-glory-god-romans-830.
[16] James 1:16–17 English Standard Version also as in the New International Version.

[17] Amy Grant, "This is My Father's World", Track #3 on *7th Heaven: Music That Inspired the Hit Television Series*, Image Entertainment, 1996, Audio CD.
[18] L. L. Larkin - Adapter, *Psalm Hymns: Dramatic, Contemplative, Singable, Recitable Psalms!,* Revised Edition, (Littleton: Capture Books, 2019), 17.

CHAPTER 3: TO TRANSFORM

[1] Stacy Horn, *Imperfect Harmony* (Chapel Hill: Algonquin Books, 2013), 1, 2.
[2] Laura Bagby, "Phillip Yancey: Hinting at God", Spiritual Life, CBN, https://www1.cbn.com/biblestudy/philip-yancey:-hinting-at-god.
[3] 2 Sam. 16:5–12 Berean Study Bible.
[4] Kenny Rogers, *The Gambler*, (Nashville: Sound Emporium, 1978), https://genius.com/Kenny-rogers-the-gambler-lyrics.
[5] "Charisma", Charisma, Wikipedia, Last modified on March 6, 2020, https://en.wikipedia.org/wiki/Charisma.
[6] Bob Deffinbaugh, "The Glory of God (Romans 8:30)," Bible.org, August 18, 2004, https://bible.org/seriespage/19-glory-god-romans-830.
[7] "Names of God", Bible Questions, Bibleinfo.com (website), 2019, https://www.bibleinfo.com/en/questions/names-of-god.
[8] Rom. 8:27–28.
[9] Phil. 4:7,9.
[10] Ibid.
[11] Phil. 4:7,9.
[12] 1 Sam. 21:10 et seq.
[13] Eccles. 3:11.
[14] Gen. 21:14–19 King James Version.
[15] Luke 18:18–24 doesn't mention Jesus' love. Mark 10:21 does.
[16] Prov. 20:5.
[17] Charles Fayette McGlashan, *History of the Donner Party: A Tragedy of the Sierra* (11th Edition), (San Francisco: A Carlisle & Co, 1918).
[18] Prov. 20:5 NIV.
[19] Ps. 78.

[20] Phil. 2:14.
[21] Phil. 4:19 New King James Version.
[22] Lam. 3:23.
[23] Ps. 51:12.
[24] Wil Pounds, "Glorification of the Christian," In "Selah", AbideInChrist.com, 2006, http://www.abideinchrist.com/selah/aug 7.html.
[25] Lynn Byk and Joseph Byk, *Mister B: Living With a 98-Year-Old Rocket Scientist,* (Littleton: Capture Books, 2016).
[26] John 15:16 NIV.
[27] L.L. Larkins-Adapter, *Psalm Hymns: Dramatic, Contemplative, Singable, Recitable Psalms!,* Revised Edition, (Littleton: Capture Books, 2019).
[28] L.L. Larkins-Adapter, *Caroling Through the Psalms,* Revised Edition, (Littleton: Capture Books, 2019).
[29] Matt. 12:35–37 Berean Study Bible.
[30] Rom. 8:30.
[31] Ezra 6:14–18.
[32] Neh. 2:17–18.
[33] Phil. 1:6 English Standard Version.

CHAPTER 4: TO COMMUNICATE

[1] Emily Crane, "'My dad is in his own world now': Glen Campbell's daughter Ashley opens up about the country legend's heartbreaking battle with Alzheimer's," DailyMail.com, Last modified June 22, 2017, https://www.dailymail.co.uk/news/article-4631278/Glen-Campbell-s-daughter-opens-Alzheimer-s-battle.html.

[2] Isa. 40:26 English Standard Version.
[3] Gen. 1:5,8.
[4] Gen. 2:19.
[5] Gen. 2:23.
[6] Matt. 7:17 New International Version.
[7] Bob Deffinbaugh, "The Glory of God (Romans 8:30)," Bible.org, August 18, 2004, https://bible.org/seriespage/19-glory-god-romans-830.
[8] Isa 55:11.

[9] Anne Rice, *Called Out of Darkness: A Spiritual Confession*, (New York: Anchor Books, 2008).

[10] Ibid.

[11] G. K. Chesterton, *The Ball and the Cross*, (Mineola: Dover Publications, 1995).

[12] Gen. 2:7; 21.

[13] Rom. 5:2.

[14] Rom. 8:24–25.

[15] Heb. 11:1.

[16] Matt. 3:17 ESV and Berean Study Bible.

[17] Heb. 4:15 ESV.

[18] Rom. 9:20–21.

CHAPTER 5: MIMIC TRUTH IN MEASURED BREATHS

[1] John 20:22 New International Version.

[2] Num. 27: 8–11.

[3] Heb. 11:1.

[4] Exod. 24:16–17.

[5] Deut. 6:8–9.

[6] Rom. 12:2 NIV.

[7] Ignatius of Loyola, *A Pilgrim's Testament: The Memoirs of Saint Ignatius of Loyola*, Translated by Parmananda R. Divarkar, (St. Louis: The Institute of Jesuit Sources, 2006).

[8] Thomas Mann Quotes, BrainyQuote.com, BrainyMedia Inc, 2019,

https://www.brainyquote.com/quotes/thomas_mann_397654, accessed December 18, 2019.

[9] Jacob Grimm and Wilhelm Grimm, *Grimm's Complete Fairy Tales,* Translated by Margaret Hunt, (San Diego: Canterbury Classics / Baker & Taylor Publishing Group, 2011), 81-86.

[10] Tonya Jewel Blessing, *The Whispering of the Willows*, (Littleton: Capture Books, 2016).

[11] Lynn Byk and Joseph Byk, *Mister B: Living With a 98-Year-Old Rocket Scientist*, (Littleton: Capture Books, 2017).

[12] John 7:37.

[13] Gen. 6:14 Berean Study Bible.

14 Exod. 20:2–17.
15 Kathy Schiffer, "Peacocks on Flannery O'Connor's Far, and in Christian Art," National Catholic Register (Blog), http://www.ncregister.com/blog/kschiffer/peacocks-on-flannery-oconners-farm-and-in-christian-art.
16 Lynn Beck, Facebook post, April 2019.
17 Matt. 4:1–4.
18 Anne Lamott, *Hallelujah Anyway*, (New York :Riverhead Books, 2017), 157.
19 Gen. 4.
20 *An Essay on the Mother of God in the Theology of Karl Barth. (Oxford: Fairacre) pp. 1–24. ISBN 0728300737.*

CHAPTER 6: FOCUS ON DETAIL
1 Auralee Arkinsly, *Darling Hedgehog Goes Down a Foxhole*, (Littleton: Capture Books, 2019).
2 Judg. 19–20:6 New King James Version.
3 Gen. 37:12–36.
4 Gen. 4:1–14.
5 Gen. 13.
6 Exod. 2.
7 Exod. 15:26 NKJV.
8 Deut. 7:12–15; 28:58–60.

9 10 Thoughts on What Truly Matters, December 6, Lisa Beebe, https://www.kcet.org/arts-entertainment/10-thoughts-on-what-truly-matters.
10 Ibid.

CHAPTER 7: FIND AND EXPLORE SEMIOTIC SURPRISES
1 "Semiotics," Semiotics, Wikipedia, last modified December 12, 2019, https://en.wikipedia.org/wiki/Semiotics.
2 Barbara Brown Taylor, *Learning to Walk in the Dark*, (New York: Harper Collins, 2015), 10.
3 Isa. 45:3 English Standard Version.
4 Taylor, 15.

[5] "Entry for holistic", Lexico.com, https://www.lexico.com/en/definition/holistic.

[6] December 29, 2015 12:00 AM ET

https://www.npr.org/2015/12/28/460731606/life-s-many-codas-maya-shankar-s-path-from-juilliard-to-the-white-house

[7] Anne Laurence, W. R. Owens, and Stuart Sim, *John Bunyan and His England 1628–1688*, 1st Edition, (New York: Bloomsbury Academic, 2003).

[8] Annie Dillard, *Pilgrim at Tinker Creek*, (New York: Harper Collins, 1974).

[9] "George MacDonald," Writing Scotland, BBC,CO.UK, 2019, https://www.bbc.co.uk/programmes/profiles/N8DKT5rH8rhHmygmpwqSl7/george-macdonald

[10] "Wife," The George MacDonald Informational Web, 2007 http://georgemacdonald.info/wife.html.

[11] C. S. Lewis, *All My Road Before Me: The Diary of C. S. Lewis, 1922–1927,* (New York: Harper Collins Publishers, 1991).

[12] J. D. Douglas, "G. K. Chesterton, the Eccentric Prince of Paradox," Christianity Today, January 8, 2001. https://www.christianitytoday.com/ct/2001/augustweb-only/8-27-52.0.html.

[13] Barbara Reynolds, *Dorothy L. Sayers: Her Life and Soul,* (New York: St. Martin's Press, 1997).

[14] Emily Gaudette, "Tolkien Director Details the Poverty That Shaped J.R.R. Tolkein's Life and LOTR," SYFY Wire, SYFY.com, May 11, 2019, https://www.syfy.com/syfywire/tolkien-director-details-the-poverty-that-shaped-jrr-tolkiens-life-and-lotr

[15] Hannah Hunnard, *The Shining Hour of Departure*, (Huntsville: Firestarter Publications, 2012), 3.

[16] Carole F. Chase, *Suncatcher: A Study of Madeleine L'Engle*, (New York: Farrar, Straus, and Giroux Publishing Company, 2001).

[17] Charmayne Hafen, *Land of Twilight*, (Littleton: Capture Books, 2019).

18 Barbara Brown Taylor, *Learning to Walk in the Dark*, (New York: Harper Collins, 2015), 90.
19 Taylor, 92.
20 Taylor, 110.
21 Exod. 17:1–6 New International Version.
22 Allen Arnold, *The Story of With*, (The Mountains of Colorado: Allen Arnold, 2016).
23 Charmayne Hafen, *Indebted: The Berkshire Dragon*, 2nd Edition, (Littleton: Capture Books, 2019),
24 Luke 13:20–21.
25 Luke 11:13.
26 Bob Deffinbaugh, "The Glory of God (Romans 8:30)," Bible.org, August 18, 2004, https://bible.org/seriespage/19-glory-god-romans-830.
27 Judg. 20:16.
28 Job 19:6.
29 Rev. 3:12 New King James Version.
30 Deut. 1:28.
31 Luke 24:13–31 NKJV.
32 Amy Pierson, Burning Heart Workshop Speaker, Denver Women's Leadership luncheon, July 2017, https://www.burning heartworkshops.com.
33 Dizzy Gillespie, "A Night in Tunisia (Interlude)", Track #1 on *Night in Tunisia: The Very Best of Dizzy Gillispie*", Bluebird / Legacy, 2006, Audio CD.
34 Isa. 44:28; 45:13 Berean Study Bible.
35 Hannah Arendt, Brainy Quotes, BrainyQuote.com, 2019, https://www.brainyquote.com/quotes/hannah_arendt 108648.
36 Matt. 27:11–26; Mark 15:1–15; Luke 23:1–25; John 19:1–22.
37 Ps. 72:10–11 New International Version.
38 Ps. 150:6 New International Version.

CHAPTER 8: NURTURE CREATIVES
1 Rom. 8:18 Berean Study Bible.
2 "Annie Sullivan," Biography, Biography.com, last modified April 12, 2019, https://www.biography.com/activist/anne-sullivan

3 Diane Andrews, *My Step Journal: 365 Days Into Intimacy with God*, (Littleton: Capture Books, 2016).

4 Tonya Jewel Blessing, *Soothing Rain: Living Water to Refresh Your Soul*, (Littleton: Capture Books, 2017).

5 Ibid.

6 Francis A. Shaeffer, *Art and the Bible*, 2nd Edition, (Downers Grove: InterVarsity Press, 2006).

7 Ibid.

8 Tonya Jewel Blessing, *The Whispering of the Willows,* (Littleton: Capture Books, 2017).

9 Ibid.

10 Eph. 4:11; 1 Cor. 12:9,28; 1 Tim 4:11–12; 2 Tim 4:2.

11 Joshua 6:1–20.

12 Luke 10:7 Berean Study Bible.

13 Gen. 30:11–13.

14 Gen. 30:30–43.

15 Lam. 3:23.

16 Lam. 3:23.

17 Deut. 5:10.

18 1 Sam. 21:18–23:29.

19 Job 1:13–22; 2:7–10 BSB.

20 Esther 4:10–7:16.

21 Gen. 37–39:20 New International Version.

22 1 Sam. 1:1–11; Gen. 29:31–30:4. In those days, it was customary for a woman to give her female servant to her spouse to obtain children if she was barren.

23 Dan. 6:1–16.

24 Dan. 3:1–23.

25 Acts 27:27–42; 2 Cor. 11:25.

26 Yaron Steinbuch, "ISIS Monsters Execute Nearly a Dozen Christians Around Christmastime," New York Post, NewYorkPost.com, December 27, 2019, https://nypost.com/2019/12/27/isis-monsters-execute-nearly-a-dozen-christians-around-christmastime. Many Christians have been beheaded due to their faith since the establishment of the first church at Antioch. As recently as Christmas this year, ISIS aligned Jihadists shot one male captive and beheaded eleven others.

---

[27] Teresa Donellan, "Genocide, Cruxification, and Rape: What Christians are Facing in the Middle East," Politics and Society, America Magazine.org, December 8, 2016, https://www.americamagazine.org/politics-society/2016/12/08/genocide-crucifixion-and-rape-what-christians-are-facing-middle-east.
As this article explains, it is often dangerous to claim to be a Christian in the Middle East.
[28] "Christian Persecution," Open Doors USA, OpenDoorsUSA.org, 2019, https://www.opendoorsusa.org/Christian-persecution.
[29] Gen. 37:25–28; Gen. 39:12–20; 41:39–43.
[30] Ruth 1:16–4:16.
[31] 1 Sam. 21:8–23:29; Acts 13:22.
[32] Esther 2:7–9:32.
[33] Judg. 4.
[34] Heb. 11:1 King James Version.
[35] Ps. 33:6–12a NIV.

CHAPTER 9: NOT ALL ART IS FOR ALL SOULS

[36] Ezek. 33:32 New King James Version.
[37] Ps. 2
[38] Rev. 3:19.
[39] Rom. 10:2–3.
[40] Ps. 127:1–2 New American Standard Version.
[41] Isa. 1:13.
[42] "Entry for agape", Lexico.com, https://www.lexico.com/en/definition/agape.
[43] 1 Cor. 7:3–5 New King James Version.
[44] Eccles 3.
[45] Exod. 20:3–5.
[46] Bishop Horsley, "Commentary on Hosea 11:2 -Graven Images," Studylight.org, 2019, https://www.studylight.org/commentary/hosea/11-2.html.
[47] Jer. 50:38–39 New Living Translation.
[48] Isa. 40:18–20 English Standard Version.
[49] Isa. 42:8 NIV.
[50] Job 1:21a.

[51] Gen. 3:7,10 ESV.
[52] Gen. 3:1.
[53] John 21:7.
[54] Isa. 47:1–3.
[55] Exod. 28.
[56] Isa. 47:2–3.
[57] Isa. 20:4.
[58] Ezek. 16:37 ESV.
[59] Rev. 3.
[60] Rev. 3.

CHAPTER 10: GOOD HUMOR IS SACRED

[1] Gal. 5:23 New King James Version.
[2] Ps. 51:12 New International Version.
[3] Gal. 5:23.

CHAPTER 11: ON A WING AND A PRAYER

[4] Rev. 22:12–14 Berean Study Bible.
[5] Prov. 1:1–7.
[6] 2 Cor. 9:9–14 Berean Study Bible.
[7] Ps. 37.
[8] Prov. 9:10 King James Version.

Bibliography

Andrews, Andrews. *My Step Journal: 365 Days Into Intimacy with God.* Littleton: Capture Books, 2016.

"Annie Sullivan." Biography. Biography.com. last modified April 12, 2019. https://www.biography.com/activist/anne-sullivan.

Arendt, Hannah. Brainy Quotes. BrainyQuote.com. 2019. https://www.brainyquote.com/quotes/hannah_are ndt_108648.

Arkinsly, Auralee. *Darling Hedgehog Goes Down a Foxhole.* Littleton: Capture Books, 2019.

Allen Arnold, *The Story of With,* (The Mountains of Colorado: Allen Arnold, 2016).

Bagby, Laura. "Phillip Yancey: Hinting at God." Spiritual Life. CBN. https://www1.cbn.com/biblestudy/philip-yancey:-hinting-at-god.

Bender, Sue. *Plain and Simple: A Woman's Journey to the Amish.* New York: HarperCollins Publishers, 1991.

"Benedictine-Values." MaterChristi. last modified 2019. https://www.materchristi.edu.au/benedictine-values.

Blessing, Tonya Jewel. *Soothing Rain: Living Water to Refresh Your Soul.* Littleton: Capture Books, 2017.

Blessing, Tonya Jewel. *The Whispering of the Willows.* Littleton: Capture Books, 2016.

Byk, Lynn and Joseph Byk. *Mister B: Living With a 98-Year-Old Rocket Scientist.* Littleton: Capture Books, 2016.

Chase, Carole F. *Suncatcher: A Study of Madeleine L'Engle.* New York: Farrar, Straus, and Giroux Publishing Company, 2001.

Chesterton, G.K.. *The Ball and the Cross.* Mineola: Dover Publications, 1995.

"Christian Persecution." Open Doors USA. OpenDoorsUSA.org. 2019. https://www.opendoorsusa.org/Christian-persecution.

Deffinbaugh, Bob. "The Glory of God (Romans 8:30)." Bible.org. August 18, 2004. https://bible.org/seriespage/19-glory-god-romans-830.

DeGraaf, Josiah. "The Reason Many Modern Christian Stories Fail." Post. Facebook.com. September 29, 2017. https://www.facebook.com/josiahdegraaf/?__tn__=%2Cd%2CP-R&eid=ARADuDbZ0wMEtYBOf-WUr_UTPUNBfv8HTJ4pLEwbpshizFvKxxiBgs2mKQpbr32NNOW3VkFN07e9DxP

Dillard, Annie. *Pilgrim at Tinker Creek.* New York: Harper Collins, 1974

Donellan, Teresa. "Genocide, Crucifixion, and Rape:
    What Christians are Facing in the Middle East."
    Politics and Society. America Magazine.org.
    December 8, 2016.
    https://www.americamagazine.org/politics-
    society/2016/12/08/genocide-crucifixion-and-
    rape-what-christians-are-facing-middle-east.

Douglas, J.D. "G. K. Chesterton, the Eccentric Prince of
    Paradox." Christianity Today. January 8, 2001.
    https://www.christianitytoday.com/ct/2001/august
    web-only/8-27-52.0.html.

Dylan, Bob. *Gotta Serve Somebody.* Sheffield: Muscle
    Shoals Sound Studios, 1979.
    https://genius.com/Bob-dylan-gotta-serve-
    somebody-lyrics.

"Entry for holistic." Lexico.com.
    https://www.lexico.com/en/definition/holistic.

"Entry for agape." Lexico.com.
    https://www.lexico.com/en/definition/agape.

Gaudette, Emily. "Tolkien Director Details the Poverty
    That Shaped J.R.R. Tolkein's Life and LOTR."
    SYFY Wire. SYFY.com. May 11, 2019.
    https://www.syfy.com/syfywire/tolkien-director-
    details-the-poverty-that-shaped-jrr-tolkiens-life-
    and-lotr

"George MacDonald." Writing Scotland. BBC,CO.UK.
    2019.
    https://www.bbc.co.uk/programmes/profiles/N8D
    KT5rH8rhHmygmpwqSl7/george-macdonald

Gillespie, Dizzy. "A Night in Tunisia (Interlude)." Track #1 on *Night in Tunisia: The Very Best of Dizzy Gillispie*." Bluebird / Legacy. 2006. Audio CD.

Grant, Amy. "This is My Father's World." Track #3 on *7th Heaven: Music That Inspired the Hit Television Series*. Image Entertainment. 1996. Audio CD.

Grimm, Jacob and Wilhelm Grimm. *Grimm's Complete Fairy Tales*. Translated by Margaret Hunt. San Diego: Canterbury Classics / Baker & Taylor Publishing Group, 2011.

Hafen, Charmayne. *Indebted: The Berkshire Dragon*. 2nd Edition. Littleton: Capture Books, 2019.

Hafen, Charmayne. *Land of Twilight*. Littleton: Capture Books, 2019.

Hunnard, Hannah. *The Shining Hour of Departure*. Huntsville: Firestarter Publications, 2012.

Ignatius, Saint of Loyola. *A Pilgrim's Testament: The Memoirs of Saint Ignatius of Loyola*. Translated by Parmananda R. Divarkar. St. Louis: The Institute of Jesuit Sources, 2006.

Joy, Kathy. *Breath of Joy - Ah Autumn*. Littleton: Capture Books, 2018.

Joy, Kathy. *Breath of Joy - Simply Summer*. Littleton: Capture Books, 2017.

Joy, Kathy. *Breath of Joy - Singing Spring*. Littleton: Capture Books, 2019.

Joy, Kathy. *Breath of Joy - Winter Whispers.* Littleton: Capture Books, 2019.

Lamott, Anne. *Hallelujah Anyway.* New York :Riverhead Books, 2017.

Larkin, L.L. - Adapter. *Caroling Through the Psalms.* Revised Edition. Littleton: Capture Books, 2019.

Larkin L.L. - Adapter. *Psalm Hymns: Dramatic, Contemplative, Singable, Recitable Psalms!.* Revised Edition. Littleton: Capture Books, 2019.

Laurence, Anne. W. R. Owens, and Stuart Sim. *John Bunyan and His England 1628-1688.* 1ˢᵗ Edition. New York: Bloomsbury Academic, 2003.

Lewis, C. S. *All My Road Before Me: The Diary of C. S. Lewis, 1922-1927.* New York: Harper Collins Publishers, 1991.

"Logos." Logos. Wikipedia. last modified on December 9, 2019. https://en.wikipedia.org/wiki/Logos.

McGlashan, Charles Fayette. *History of the Donner Party: A Tragedy of the Sierra.* 11ᵗʰ Edition. San Francisco: A Carlisle & Co, 1918.

"Names of God." Bible Questions. Bibleinfo.com (website). 2019. https://www.bibleinfo.com/en/questions/names-of-god.

Pierson, Amy. Burning Heart Workshop Speaker. Denver Women's Leadership luncheon. July 2017. https://www.burning heartworkshops.com.

Pounds, Wil. "Glorification of the Christian." In "Selah." AbideInChrist.com. 2006. http://www.abideinchrist.com/selah/aug7.html.

Reynolds, Barbara. *Dorothy L. Sayers: Her Life and Soul.* New York: St. Martin's Press, 1997.

Rice, Anne. *Called Out of Darkness: A Spiritual Confession.* New York: Anchor Books, 2008.

Rogers, Kenny. *The Gambler.* Nashville: Sound Emporium, 1978. https://genius.com/Kenny-rogers-the-gambler-lyrics.

Schiffer, Kathy. "Peacocks on Flannery O'Conner's Farm, and in Christian Art." National Catholic Register (Blog). http://www.ncregister.com/blog/kschiffer/peacocks-on-flannery-oconners-farm-and-in-christian-art.

"Science". Anatomy in Leonardo da Vinci. N.P.. https://www.leonardo-da-vinci.ch/science.

"Semiotics." Semiotics. Wikipedia. last modified December 12, 2019. https://en.wikipedia.org/wiki/Semiotics.

Shaeffer, Francis A. *Art and the Bible.* 2nd Edition. Downers Grove: InterVarsity Press, 2006.

Steinbuch, Yaron. "ISIS Monsters Execute Nearly a Dozen Christians Around Christmastime." New York Post. NewYorkPost.com. December 27, 2019. https://nypost.com/2019/12/27/isis-monsters-execute-nearly-a-dozen-christians-around-christmastime.

Taylor, Barbara Brown. *Learning to Walk in the Dark*. New York: Harper Collins, 2015.

"Thomas Mann Quotes." BrainyQuote.com, BrainyMedia, Inc. 2019, https://www.brainyquote.com/quotes/thomas_mann_397654, accessed December 18, 2019.

Walker, W. L.. "Entry for Cunning." In *The International Standard Bible Encyclopedia*. edited by James Orr, N.P..1915. http://classic.studylight.org/enc/isb/view.cgi?number=T2446.

Weber, Max. *The Theory of Social and Economic Organization*. Translated by A. M. Henderson and Talcott Parsons. New York: The Free Press, 1964.

"Wife." The George MacDonald Informational Web. 2007. http://georgemacdonald.info/wife.html.

Additional Reading

Other works that encourage Christian mentors and authors to tap into the expansive symbolism of God's Word:

- Peterson, Andrew (2019) *Adorning the Dark* B&H Publishing Group, 200 pages. ISBN:9781535949026

- Smith, James Byron (2017) *The Magnificent Story: Uncovering a Gospel of Beauty, Goodness, and Truth* (Apprentice Resources) IVP Books, 192 pages. ISBN 9780830846368

- Outcalt, Todd (2017) *The Seven Deadly Virtues: Temptations In Our Pursuit of Goodness* IVP Books, 160 pages. ISBN 9781543614077

- Allender, Dan, and Longman, Tremper, (2015) *The Cry of the Soul: How Our Emotions Reveal Our Deepest Questions About God* NavPress, 272 pages. ISBN 9781576831809

- Smith, David I (2015) *Teaching and Christian Imagination* Wm. B. Eerdmans Publishing Co., 208 pages. ISBN 9780802873231

- Haidt, Jonathan (2011) *The Righteous Mind: Why Good People are Divided by Politics and Religion* Vintage; Reprint, 528 pages. ISBN 978-0307455772

- Thompson, Curt (2010) *Anatomy of the Soul: Surprising Connections between Neuroscience and Spiritual Practices That Can Transform Your Life and Relationships,* Tyndale Momentum, 304 pages. ISBN 978-1414334158

- Brink, Jonathan (2010) *Discovering The God Imagination: Reconstructing A Whole New Christianity* CreateSpace Independent Publishing Platform, 306 pages. ISBN 9781453650745

- Dalton, Russell W. (2003) *Faith Journey Through Fantasy Lands: A Christian Dialogue With Harry Potter, Star Wars, and the Lord of the Rings.* Minneapolis: Augsburg Fortress Publishers, 160 pages. ISBN 9780806645711

- Ryken, Leland (2002) *The Christian Imagination: The Practice of Faith in Literature and Writing* (Writers' Palette Book) Shaw Books, 480 pages. ISBN 9780877881230

- Bell, James Scott (2009) *The Art of War for Writers: Fiction Writing Strategies, Tactics, and Exercises;* Writer's Digest Books *ISBN:* 978-1582975900

- May, Stephen (1998) *Stardust and Ashes : Science Fiction in Christian Perspective.* n.p.: Society for promoting Christian knowledge, 160 pages. ISBN 9780281051045

- Palmer, Bernard (1968) *Jim Dunlap and the Wingless Plane.* Chicago: Moody Press. ISBN 0-8024-4302-8

- Schmemann, Alexander (1998) *For the Life of the World;* St Vladimirs Seminary Press, 186 pages. ISBN 978-0881416176

LAURA BARTNICK appreciates a good
conversation about the subject of
creativity. She works for Capture Books
as an acquisition editor. Social Media
sites: @ CaptureBooks on Facebook,
Pinterest, Instagram, Goodreads, and
LinkedIn. Please consider sharing how
BEING CREATIVE may have helped you
or revealed something to you in some way.
Tell a friend or leave a review with your
favorite book review platform.

Thank you!

Being Creative

Lightning Source UK Ltd.
Milton Keynes UK
UKHW020932220421
382374UK00001B/15